HEART
Rhythms

Also by Jasmine Leigh Morse

Heart Rhythms: A Guided Journal for Thriving in Singleness

HEART
Rhythms

SURVIVING SINGLENESS
with
FAITH, KNOW-HOW, & GRIT

JASMINE LEIGH MORSE

E.M. Williams Publishing

Baltimore

E.M. Williams Publishing
Baltimore, Maryland
Copyright © 2020 Jasmine Leigh Morse

Portions of this book's introduction were previously published. Grateful acknowledgment is made to *Blavity* for permission to reprint the following article by Jasmine Leigh Morse originally published in *Blavity*: "How I Found Love Once I Stopped Trying to Schedule It," copyright © 2018 by *Blavity*. Reprinted by permission of *Blavity*.

Unless otherwise indicated, all Scripture quotations are taken from the Holy Bible, New Living Translation, copyright © 1996, 2004, 2015 by Tyndale House Foundation. Used by permission of Tyndale House Publishers, a Division of Tyndale House Ministries, Carol Stream, Illinois 60188. All rights reserved.

Scripture quotations taken from the Amplified® Bible (AMP), Copyright © 2015 by The Lockman Foundation Used by permission. www.Lockman.org.

Scripture quotations marked MSG are taken from *THE MESSAGE*, copyright © 1993, 2002, 2018 by Eugene H. Peterson. Used by permission of NavPress. All rights reserved. Represented by Tyndale House Publishers, a Division of Tyndale House Ministries.

This book recounts events in the life of Jasmine L. Leigh Morse according to the author's recollection and perspective. While all the stories are true, names are omitted and identifying details have been changed to protect the privacy of those involved.

Paperback ISBN: 978-1-7358080-0-0
eBook ISBN: 978-1-7358080-1-7

Book Design: Make Your Mark Publishing Solutions
Author Photo: Naaman Brown

For information about the author, speaker requests, or media inquiries, please email: info@jasmineleighmorse.com. To connect with the author on social media, use the hashtag #HeartRhythms and like, share, subscribe, or comment:

Instagram: @drjasmineleighmorse
Facebook: Dr. Jasmine Leigh Morse
Twitter: @drjleighmorse
LinkedIn: Jasmine Leigh Morse, PhD

*For My Mom. For My Sisters.
For her, she, and we who survive, transform,
and live to tell universal stories.*

CONTENTS

Introduction

I've spent my academic career studying the lives of exceptional, transformative black women. I love unpacking their lives in ways that reveal their ability to ascend and transcend negative stereotypes. I've dedicated my personal reading lists to autobiographies, biographies, and historical references about such women. In these stories, I was awakened to common trends that resonate among black women within every field, from arts and entertainment, to business, media, and government. This innate transformational power enabled women like Josephine Baker, Octavia E. Butler, Madame C.J. Walker, Shirley Chisolm, Maya Angelou, Oprah Winfrey, and many others to overcome stifling circumstances that should've buried the essence of who we know them to be today. Their creative, resilient power is so compelling and recognizable that they come to the forefront in their respective industries and in some ways, offer a blueprint for others to follow. As I've studied the lives of women, I've had the pleasure of examining the exceptional qualities of those who inspire me, without ever looking within myself to do the same. *Isn't it so interesting that women can celebrate the value and contributions of other women without searching ourselves to do the same?*

It wasn't until I approached my wedding date with giddy excitement that I paused within the haze of wedding planning to reflect on my transformative story. What I found was . . . I, too, have qualities that are worth acknowledging and celebrating. And so, it's within these pages that I offer snippets of my journey as a single woman. Although I've turned my research lens on myself to unpack my story, I don't assume that you'll automatically understand thoughts that have swirled around in my head for some time now. At times, I'll fold into my narrative, context for the sake of clarity, with the hope that I've communicated my thoughts well—though not as blatantly as they came to mind. *This is a goal any writer should seek to achieve with skill.*

Before you dive in, here's the framework for understanding what I've had time to think about and understand about myself: Every facet of life has a rhythm, a repeated pattern that guides our lives. For me, the life rhythm is shaped by societal and familial influences, environment, or day-to-day activities. Think about your daily routine, work schedule, workout regimen, weekly meal plan, or everyday to-do list. All of these things have a pace, whether fast or slow. Just like the rhythm of music, these things also have a particular sound associated with them. Can you hear the sound of co-workers saying, "Good morning," as they walk through the office every morning? Can you hear the sound of a runner on the treadmill? Can you hear the sound of a mother preparing dinner after a long day at work, while trying to help her children with homework? These are some of the life rhythms that repeat with movement and sound. Yet, when life is interrupted by trauma, stress, busyness, or anything in between, we are forced to recognize that . . . our movements . . . our sounds can be thrown off. Routines start to slip. Chores and day-to-day obligations suffer from lack of attention. The interruptions of life take central focus and sometimes consume the mind with an array of emotions.

Even with that, I believe the rhythm of life finds its pulse in the heart rhythm. Just as our physical heart gives life to our body and serves as the main organ that pumps blood, so too does the heart rhythm help sustain the life rhythm. If the heart stops beating, life stops. If the heartbeat is irregular, the body doesn't function properly. For me, the heart rhythm sets the pace for our body in ways that speak to our emotional health. When our life rhythm is hit with unexpected challenges—heartbreak, job loss, or sickness, the heart responds to an emotional signal from the brain when feelings of disappointment, frustration, fear, or anger impact our lives. I believe that the heart rhythm gives us inward signs about our feelings—sadness, happiness, or contentment—concerning life, people, and things. When life's challenges cause those emotions to elevate the heart rate to a fast pace, the rapid heartbeat could signal many things, including excitement, joy, and fear.

Science says, an irregular heartbeat or heart rhythm can be caused by fright, shock, or stress, causing the heart to beat too fast or too slow. Although I'd experienced a rapid heart rate that signaled the joys of life or mere movie-night fright when watching a Netflix thriller, understanding my heart rhythm needed a bit more analysis. My elevated heart rate came from an emotional place that caused anxiety and fear to speed up my heartbeat to an erratic pace. I know now that I lived with an emotional heart arrhythmia, an intense, fast-paced heart rate that was driven by a desire to get married. I began to recognize a repeated pattern in how I operated and felt in romantic relationships with men, and I found the source of my heart irregularity within my family history. From the onset of my birth, fatherlessness and the tragedy of generational patterns among the women in my family ill-equipped me to attract and develop relationships with men who added value to my life. For me, childhood trauma, teenage pressures, heartbreak, and youthful growing pains left me challenged in my early adult dating life. Therefore, I struggled with steadying myself in singleness and foolishly thought getting married would fill voids, needs, wants, and desires.

Likewise, the rapid cadence of my 20-year-old heartbeat drove my actions, relationships, and made me anxious, fearful—even disappointed. Personal declarations about how I'd be married after earning a master's degree were a part of my edict. When and where I developed this false sense of reality, I don't know. I mapped out when I wanted to finish school and purchase my first home. I also set deadlines for my career goals, future marriage, starting a family, and the list goes on. And of course, it didn't help when I had—shall I say—seasoned women hounding me about when I was getting married. *When are you getting married? How are things going with so and so? How much longer do you have in school? Girl, you are almost 30.* Sheesh, talk about overwhelming! My identity . . . my personhood couldn't be shaped by whether I did or didn't have a romantic relationship. Like, who made that up? Seriously! But, what I know for sure is if my plan had come to fruition, yeah—that would not have been a good thing.

While my model of womanhood was shaped by great women, I had no foundational examples of successful romantic relationships to inspire me or aspire to in my life. Let me take a step back to explain. I'm a product of Baltimore, Maryland but born in Silver Spring, Maryland in the 1980s. A county girl they say . . . that's how kids I grew up with described girls who lived in the county and attended Baltimore County schools. I don't recall whether categorizing city and county girls into two different groups was learned through adult conversations or whether it was something that we kids started and it became socially acceptable. I have no idea whether the defining elements were based on girl groups from diverse backgrounds like those in the hit movie, *Bring It On*, starring Kirsten Dunst and Gabrielle Union. I just know that even as a teenager, the distinction didn't feel right to me. For me, the expression, depending on who was saying it, seemed to favor one group over the other. Somehow, even as a kid, I was being conditioned to understand who I was based on a type of category that started with my peers.

My coming-of-age story was influenced by social constructs that date back centuries. At times, it was somewhat impossible to escape the stereotypes set by society for black women and girls. Whether presented in media, school, or in my environment, societal assumptions could've led me to believe that there were no more than three options for me—welfare, single motherhood, or career-driven, angry black woman, none leading to a happy marriage and family. Few women in my family escaped the prescribed "options." My mother was no different. She was a single mother of four but also a career-driven accountant who later earned her law degree. Yet, my mother and grandmother went to great lengths to affirm and encourage me to look beyond what I later learned were stereotypes. They wanted me to make the best decisions for my life, using the life lessons they taught me as a gauge. Together, they made me believe I could do anything I set out to do. *Even when I face challenges to date, I can hear my mother saying, "You can do anything you put your mind to."* They exposed me to my ancestral history, the arts, books about African princesses, black dolls, and the importance of hard work and education. All of which gave me the confidence I needed to pursue my dreams.

I recognize now that I'm an echo from the time of my foremothers who faced many struggles as they warred against external societal forces: living through slavery, Reconstruction, and Jim Crow laws, all while being black and a woman. Though they survived many things, I can't help but wonder how they managed their heart rhythms as single mothers who coped with traumas after divorce, abuse, and rape. In some instances, they faced all of these devastating circumstances throughout their lives. And yet, they all found strength and courage to triumph. Though I can't fathom how they carried the trauma of their pasts in silence. Even though they didn't talk to me about the details, I observed the effects of trauma through their actions and behaviors.

I'm grateful for the strength of the women all around me because I'm also the product of an absentee father. Despite the childhood pain of growing up without my biological father, I must acknowledge the stepfather who was gifted to me during my early years. He never made me feel like I wasn't his child, even after he and my mom separated. *I've grown to cherish his presence and love him more and more as I get older.* Through my biological father, I'm a product of West Africa, a blend of Nigeria and Sierra Leone by way of Freetown. The richness of his bloodline runs through my veins and has shown up in many ways, although we didn't start building a relationship until my mid-twenties.

Much of who I am was shaped by the single women in my life. They managed to offer me a life filled with rich love, Christian values, creativity, wisdom, and examples of strength. Because of their influence, I'm a third-generation college graduate, second-generation entrepreneur, and all-around survivor of many challenges. They showed me how to succeed and overcome obstacles as a single woman. Yet, if I wanted to embrace a healthy romantic relationship with a man, I needed to look elsewhere. I looked for love in all the wrong places. Therein, I found my problem.

Societal stigmas coupled with my self-imposed standards caused the rapid cadence of my 20-year-old heartbeat. I admit it. I didn't survive singleness well. I was stuck in a world that began with "Once upon a time" and ended with, "And they lived happily ever after." My pathway from girl-hood to womanhood was blurred by my negative outlook. I couldn't imagine who I was authentically becoming without a Prince Charming in my life. I grew up without good examples of healthy male-female relationships and marriages. What was I to do with no relationship role model? I used my creativity to draw my own conclusions. What a pitfall that had me living in a fantasy world.

Between my goals, wants, desires, and the perceptions of others, it's a wonder I survived. But, I didn't make it without the stress that led to bouts of depression. Sure, I'd accomplished a lot by setting short and long-term goals. But, the pressure I placed on myself to have a successful career, and all that I had imagined as a child, didn't allow me to recognize all of the wonderful moments in my life. I graduated high school at 16, owned my own home by 28, and earned multiple degrees before 30. Yet, I was speeding through life using an idealistic schedule and fighting to attain what I thought was my peak—career, husband, and family.

Looking back, I can say that I was most often thrown off beat by disappointments in relationships—nothing else really. Challenges in school or work didn't shake me and neither did managing my finances during times of hardship. It was men. Why have failed relationships caused so much trauma in my life? I consider myself a pretty unshakable person, but when a relationship failed, I painfully crashed like cymbals in a middle school band.

Truth is . . . I was an emotional wreck for most of my

twenties, especially after a breakup. No, really. I think I gave my mother the blues. Whenever I was having an emotional meltdown, complete with sobbing and crying on the floor or in my bed all night, she was there, whether through her physical presence or by phone. Though not solely relegated to this time, every common symptom associated with pre-menstrual syndrome knocked on my door like clockwork every month, especially depression, anxiety, and mood swings. It was as if all the emotion associated with wanting to feel loved and get married was exacerbated during that time. Overwhelming feelings of dread and fear about my future consumed my days and especially my nights. So, I clung to my mother for support.

I'm so thankful, now, that I lived at home with my mother during that time. There were days when my mother found me curled up in a ball on my bedroom floor, wrapped in a blanket, sobbing about my life. For hours, I cried over the potential loss of my college boyfriend, who at the time I was still dating. Somehow I found myself crying over the thought of him breaking up with me. I wept over loneliness. I wept over past hurts. I wept over not feeling pretty enough. I wept for anything that didn't seem to align with my "happily ever after" and all those fanciful thoughts I created for myself. My mother did what most church-going Christian mothers would do. She prayed and laid hands on me often, as she offered fervent prayers to the Lord. She challenged me to read and pray the scriptures about faith, our inheritance as believers in Christ, and hope and confidence in God. She challenged me to think and speak positive affirmations about my future. I was challenged to change my way of thinking. My mother prayed with me until I learned to pray for myself. I spent many days on the floor in my bedroom weeping. One day, I made a choice to get up off the floor and never return. Most of all, prayer and affirmations caused me to change my mindset and reflect on the origin of my pain.

It was not until my last failed relationship that I actually took a step back to understand why I fell so hard after a breakup. In retrospect, I was attracting men who were mirror images of the worst parts of my being—men who were rejected by their fathers or became replacements for my own father. Then there were those I dated who were overly emotional or filled with so much childhood hurt that it was hard to get past their hard exteriors. Whether they had characteristics that resembled my father's, I will never know. I can only acknowledge that I was drawn to men who represented the most complicated parts of my being. Likewise, I realized what was blocking me from allowing a healthy relationship to enter my life. It was me—my hurt, my pain, my unforgiveness, my rejection, my abandonment, my low self-esteem—me. All that complicated stuff in me.

Even though there was so much right about who I was becoming, the complicated parts of my being attracted everything wrong. Sure, the guys I dated played a role. And of course, the fatherless child played a part in the narrative. But, I could only accept and resolve my own issues. When I began to admit that I was blocking myself from the future I desired, I found out that I didn't love the "hims" the way I thought I did . . . point-blank. Of course, I loved things about them like their character traits, potential, and looks, along with the common interests we shared. But, when I shifted my mind toward self-reflection, self-love, and healing, I was able to literally change the pace of my heart rhythm. Once I acknowledged what I was doing wrong, I began to stand in my truth. I prayed. I forgave. I believed. I took a breath. I slowed down. I healed. I lived. I acknowledged all the fathers I had, despite the one who left. I accepted my placement and position in life, despite what I hoped to attain and become. Then, I was able to celebrate life and my future on a whole new beat.

It was sometime around 30 that my heart rhythm changed its tempo and slowed to a more reasonable pace. It was on the downbeat that I was able to acknowledge that I didn't love all the "hims" at all. I traded a life driven by a timeline for a purpose-driven life that not only included a career, husband, and family, but also a new awareness about what I was supposed to do with my time while I waited. For me, true happiness and wholeness was a journey that shifted me from fledgling, idealistic views about the meaning of success in life. I learned that growing up was a transformative process that, coupled with education and life experiences, would naturally evolve over time. When my heart rhythm changed, my pulse changed. It was then that I found a new pace that allowed time and attraction to meet on the same note, and amongst all the "hims" was the one him whose cadence matched mine.

So, 35 was my number. I thought I'd get married by 25 or no later than 30, but I didn't meet my husband until I was 35. We met in September 2016 in Washington, D.C. at the 46th Annual Legislative Conference Congressional Black Caucus. We happened upon each other at the close of the Emerging Leaders Luncheon and spent the entire event weekend together amongst friends. By the end of the weekend, we'd exchanged numbers and walked away from one another, not knowing that nearly two years later we'd be married. Our story is not like most. No, I wouldn't call it love at first sight. I would, however, frame our story as a destiny encounter that allowed us to meet just before we reached the climaxes of our individual stories. He proposed in September 2018, and we were married in May 2019.

In the months, weeks, and days leading up to my wedding day, I found that I had a lot of thoughts about my journey as a single woman, and I found solace in expressing them through social media posts. I'm a lover of words. My entire childhood was complete with summer reading lists and self-expression through poetry. I carried that same passion into my education and since then, it has shown up in my career, at times, unexpectedly. So, when we received our engagement photos, I decided to find a meaningful way to share our photos. I took to Facebook and Instagram, as many others do, to share my #surviningsingleness posts for eight weeks. I found my weekly posts to be cathartic. Moments I never really shared openly became a platform for other women and, surprisingly, other men, who seemed to really want to know and discuss what I had to say each week. I cannot count the number of conversations or direct messages I received from people expressing their connection to my social media posts. I was most touched by the women who expressed real emotion or, in their words, "cried real tears," and who could identify with my personal stories of fatherlessness or heartbreak. I felt encouraged and sought with every post to be transparent. While the social media posts were helping me, I had no idea they would make such a positive impact on others.

Although I've attended my fair share of women's empowerment group meetings, conferences, and girl power brunches, for me, there was still an undercurrent in the world around me. I felt like I was wearing a scarlet letter 'S' for single, as if being single was the worst possible outcome in life. I, like many other women, believed this lie, whether consciously or unconsciously. How was I to successfully live as a single woman, if everything around me suggested that marriage was the ultimate goal? So, I was surviving singleness because I was combatting societal stigmas and the pressure I placed on myself to get married. Sure, surviving is defined as having endured, lived through, or outlived something but that's exactly what I had to learn how to do. I had to learn how to survive in singleness because being single almost came across like it was a curse. It felt like everything I set out to accomplish was overshadowed by marriage. Casual conversations with married girlfriends were redirected to who was dating. Or, if I was dating, they'd want to know how picky I was being. It just seemed like the people around me believed that there was nothing beyond marriage for women.

Let me be clear. I don't believe there is a prescription for surviving singleness, whether there is a desire for marriage or not. Nor do I believe that there's a surefire way to get to the altar and build the family of your dreams. However, I do think that learning from the experiences of others can offer personal insights about how to navigate life. If marriage is a by-product of that newfound insight and understanding, great. I've also learned that everything meant to be will happen within the proper time. Because for far too long, I was encouraged to subscribe to a formula for how to get a man and start a family. *If I do X, then XYZ will happen.* And, I believe the formula was a part of my problem. *Go to school . . . wear this . . . no, wear that. Straighten your hair . . . no girl, some men love natural hair. Don't be too bossy . . . And, don't be too timid. Make sure you finish school before you get married.* Simply put, it was too much pressure. Everyone has their own path in life. Yet, I subscribed to the path set before me—school, maybe some college, career, husband, and children—before I had a chance to understand myself. Each of my married friends has wonderfully different stories about how they met and married their husbands. I also have friends who enjoy their freedom and don't wish to be married or have children. And then, there are some who fall somewhere in between: wanting marriage but not wanting children. I think the part I missed growing up was understanding that my path didn't have to mirror anyone else's. While it took me years to break free from ideals about marriage, my path was mine to own without feeling rushed or made to feel less than because I didn't have a husband and children at 35. Period.

With *Heart Rhythms*, what you'll find is a compilation of linked essays, based in the theme **heart rhythms**, which originated as a journal entry in 2015. Later, the theme evolved into an article that was published in 2018. With time, I was able to sit with the idea a bit more . . . hence this book title. With this book, I aim to add to conversations about women and singleness. I've written from my perspective as a black female who didn't marry until 37 and to boot just one week before my 38th birthday. While this book is 95% based on my personal stories, the remaining 5% reflects concepts that I thought were worth looking a little deeper into with some research. I believe there are a number of topics where readers will be provoked to reflect on their lives, while also finding advice—not a formula—nestled within the pages. Although I don't claim to be a relationship expert, I do own a set of experiences that may help women understand their relationships. I've written this book with the everyday reader in mind and have taken great strides to use practical concepts that add context and value to my life lessons and insights. I also include funny and fun stories in order to sprinkle humor within the pages that at times triggered deep emotion during the writing process.

That said, this book is about how I managed my heart rhythms as a single woman who desired marriage, when I wanted and how I wanted it. It exposes my growing pains and battles with disappointment, as I struggled to understand who I was and who I was becoming. It also revels in celebrating growth and development that led to a sustainable, healthy outlook and new pathway for my life. Through the process of reshaping and reinventing my identity, I found myself similarly among other transformative women. I discovered the power and capacity within myself to shift the direction of my life and steady my heart rhythm through—

- Faith: complete trust in God to help guide me through a transformative healing process;

- Know-how: use of practical tips, tools, and resources to facilitate my process; and

- Grit: ability to face and deal with deep hurt and trauma from my past with passion and persistence, and in service of my purpose and long-term goals.

So, here I am with this work, baring my heart and soul with the hope that women will be encouraged to live a life in pursuit of positive purpose and destiny. It's also my sincere hope that women are able to learn from my personal stories in ways that lead them to find and embrace authentic happiness, wholeness, and healing. If I'm able to share a glimpse of what I've hidden in my heart to ponder alone, I offer this book to other women who aim to not only survive singleness but thrive in singleness, even if they desire marriage and it never happens. Let me say that again—even if they desire marriage and it never happens.

As a single woman, I heard statistics for years about the percentage of single women or increasing divorce rates. Though that data was unpleasant to hear at times, I'd find myself grabbing my cell phone to google more exact data about marriage. I'm not sure if I was rejecting a future that included singleness and divorce, or just needed to see the data for myself. But, what I learned was consistent with what I saw among my family and friends' relationships. *Pew Research* reported that "the number of Americans living with an unmarried partner reached about 18 million in 2016, up 29% since 2007," which means that people are opting to live together before marriage, if they decide to marry at all. U.S. Census Bureau data highlighted by *Pew Research* stated that, "The median age at first marriage reached its highest point on record: 30 years for men and 28 years for women in 2018." These statistics were staggering to me and could make the strongest person feel hopeless about getting married or having a successful marriage.

Although I never lived my life based on statistics, at one point during my singleness, I began to have some real conversations with myself because thoughts about marriage were consuming my mind. Without acknowledging any documented research, the reality is, not everyone who wants to get married will get married. There are also those who will divorce and find a lasting relationship with perhaps the second or third marriage. With what I knew to be a reality in mind, at least in my environment, I needed to turn my attention away from marriage to finding my sense of self and my greater purpose in life, despite the promise of marriage or not.

Part 1

ONCE UPON A TIME

ONE

Sleeping Beauty

I lied. *I mentioned early on that I'm direct.* So yeah, I lied to myself often. I also let other people lie to me. And, although it came in different forms and by different names in my life, trauma spoke through my dreams and negative thoughts and lied, too. I was miseducated about singleness and so were those in my circle of friends and community.

For countless years, the persistent lies about singleness have exacerbated the emotions of women and even girls around the globe. You may not agree with me, but I believe that there's quite an epidemic that's encouraged women and girls to seek marriage, sometimes even before they've grasped the essence of their own identities. I'm sure we can all agree that there's been a narrative perpetuated about singleness that's founded on some really false ideologies that need to be torn down. And so, here we are, still earnestly needing to dismantle ingrained factoids that cause women to adopt someone else's personal truths as their own. I, for one, refused to be trapped by the thoughts, opinions, and fears of others. This idea that marriage is the highest accomplishment for women still flows as an undercurrent in society, despite all the cutting-edge successes of women around the world. No matter how many degrees are earned . . . no matter how many op-eds and books are published . . . no matter how large the investment portfolio . . . no matter how many C-Suite appointments or anything in between, the question still remains—*When are you getting married?*

For me, the problem was . . . those lies made me my own worst enemy. I was a type of "Sleeping Beauty" waiting for Prince Charming to come, kiss me, and save me. In reality, though, the only person who could wake me up and save me . . . was me. The miseducation of singleness buried personal and cultural untruths in my psyche that could've derailed my future if I let them. I didn't recognize until late in my twenties that the real work that I needed to do to prepare for marriage had much more to do with me and less to do with how soon and when I'd meet my future husband.

Me

I wasn't ready to get married when I thought I was. Despite the claims to my girlfriends and prayers to God about my desires for a husband, I wasn't ready. How could I have been when I was an angry, mean girl with insecurities, unforgiveness, and feelings of rejection and abandonment driving my day-to-day interactions and decisions? *Whew, that felt really good to get that off my chest.*

I remember when my mother told me that I was angry. She just blurted it out, right in the middle of a conversation. "Jasmine, you're angry. The way you look at people . . . the way you look at me sometimes. You're angry." Talk about a gut punch. She was right, and I respected her role in my life enough to listen and do some self-reflection. Anger showed up, not only in my demeanor but also in my words. And yes, I'm the girl who will say what everybody is thinking when they don't have the courage to say it. There is, however, a difference between direct transparency and being mean.

I wasn't happy with myself or circumstances in life, but that didn't make my actions right. I was angry because I wanted my life to be different, although honestly, I had a really good life. At twenty-something, I'd imagined the life that I wanted. When real life didn't measure up, I was sad, disappointed, and even angry. I wanted my father. I wanted my husband when I told God I wanted him. I consistently dwelled on everything that was going wrong in my life, while also thinking about how unhappy I was. I wanted my life to match the timeline I created for it, and when it didn't, I became afraid of my future. Truth is . . . the most complicated parts of my being left me angry and anxious all at once. It's not an excuse; it's the truth.

Therefore, I was attracting men that were the mirror images of all the stuff that I buried and never wanted to face. But, I faced myself when I met men who held a mirror up to my own identity. I was attracting what was in me.

I'm no psychologist or scientist, but I do know the Law of Attraction is real. For years, theorists have explained that the Law of Attraction is this ability to attract and/or will positive or negative things into our lives by the power of the mind. It's this ability to shape your world with your thoughts. I think speaking positive affirmations, vision boarding, or writing 5-10 year plans are great tools that help get us closer to the lives we envision for ourselves. But, when my mind was filled and even overwhelmed by negative thoughts about me and my future, framing and mounting my vision board on the wall was of no use to me.

For as he thinks in his heart, so is he. (Proverbs 23:7 [AMP])

Unless I changed my mind, my world would never change. I attracted positive things in my life when it came to everything else except men. Feelings of rejection and abandonment gained access into my life when my father left me and my mother. It was at that moment that I knew disappointment, heartbreak, and rejection, leaving me to grow up with mistrust and unforgiveness to help shape my identity. When all those emotions and feelings festered and collided, my world, community, and mindset suffered. As a child, I suffered through a deep hurt that grew with time. How could I have shaped a coherent identity with the trauma of abandonment apparent so early in my childhood? Evidence of childhood trauma surfaced through the notes I wrote my mother as a child asking her if she loved me. Or, the way I often cried myself to sleep to find comfort even when I didn't know why I was crying. It was even more apparent with every breakup I experienced in a relationship or when the slightest encounter with someone triggered real emotions.

As I grew older, I began to question myself after a breakup, which later helped me realize that I based my identity and self-worth on how a man treated me. Insecurities. *Am I slim enough? Am I pretty enough? What did I do wrong?* Those are the types of questions I'd ask myself while dating, especially in my twenties. I'm a pretty confident person when it comes to school, work, and even my talents. But, I carried feelings of rejection with me into my dating life, which stemmed from feeling abandoned by my father.

So, when I questioned myself about men—*Why did he leave me? Why didn't he want me?* It was really the little girl in me screaming, *"Daddy, why did you leave me? Daddy, why didn't you want me? Daddy, do you love me?"* My fear of being rejected, left, or abandoned with no notice caused me to live in a world that consumed my thoughts. This made me believe that all men would eventually walk away from me. And a few did just that . . . they'd say, "I don't want this anymore," or, just walk away without notice or warning.

I also attracted men who were overly emotional. Chile, one guy seemed like he cried more about his life than I did about mine! Both of us couldn't be overly emotional. *Dude!* I encountered the angry, rejected man too. He wasn't angry or aggressive toward me, but he was mad all the time about everything, particularly about being abandoned by his parents. Looking back, I sensed that he could've become aggressive or physically abusive toward me, if the relation-ship had continued. Sheesh, that was a lot for a woman in her twenties to handle while trying to graduate from college, navigate life, and start a career. So, I lied to myself about being ready for marriage when I wasn't ready at all. There was much to be done and that started with me and my emotional wellness.

It

Trauma has a name and a voice. Sometimes it spoke just as loud as the voices of people in my life. I talk a lot about the trauma and residual effects of fatherlessness and abandon-ment. But, for some, there are other unresolved traumatic experiences like molestation, sexual assault, and even physi-cal abuse that can negatively affect the potential for sustain-ing romantic relationships. For me, its name was abortion. It spoke to me loud and clear and caused me, for a time, to live trapped by its sting.

I felt mild cramping in my abdomen when I woke up in what seemed to be the tiniest medical room. I was still filled with deep emotion from the overflow of tears that I shed before being put to sleep to abort my baby. It was my decision to move forward with the procedure despite being urged by my boyfriend at the time not to move forward. Even though he pleaded with me for weeks not to get an abortion, I'd made up my mind just as soon as I took the pregnancy test to confirm. He refused to give me the $400 I needed to have the procedure, but that didn't matter. I had the money. I was an 18-year-old sophomore in college, and a baby didn't fit into my life plan. Yet, nothing could've prepared me for the experiences post-abortion that ensued moments, days, weeks, months, and years later.

With light tapping on my right hand, I began to wake up after being put to sleep. I was surrounded by a doctor, nurse, and surgical tech urging me to sit upright. I sat up on the surgical table in full view of the vacuum aspiration suction machine, where I immediately zeroed in on the remains of the child that I decided to abort. A clear container held the choice I made. I was gently urged off the table with tears streaming down my face.

Still in pain, I shuffled to the recovery room with the help of a nurse who guided me to one of what seemed to be 15 or so beds lined against the wall, with no more than 30 inches between each bed. I was one of three women in the recovery room that afternoon. I lay there in the bed, curled in a ball on my right side. I was holding my stomach with both hands, crying, and moaning, not only because I was in pain but also because I kept visualizing the content of the suction machine where I left my baby. I rocked back and forth, weeping and whispering to myself, "I killed my baby," over and over again. The more I thought about it . . . the more I cried. I was the last one to leave the recovery room.

Before I was left alone, a young lady who looked to be in little to no pain stopped and turned back toward me as she walked out of the door and said, "This is my third one. It gets easier after the first time. You'll be fine." I was shocked. I hadn't known of anyone at the time who had one abortion.

I never forgot that encounter with her. I was sure of one thing when I left that recovery room; I had no intention of returning to that facility or any other like it.

It took me more than 30 minutes to recover physically and emotionally from my experience. It took many years for me to forgive myself for what I had done and for disappointing my mother. *I can still see the look of disappointment on my mother's face when she was told I was pregnant.* I was there when a family friend told her; I couldn't bring myself to do it. My boyfriend at the time told a mutual friend, who tried to get me to change my mind about the abortion. When I didn't, the family friend called my mother and asked her to come over as soon possible. She likely felt the sense of urgency in their voice. She came to where we all were right away. Just as soon as she walked in the door, they told her I was pregnant. I couldn't. Instead, I wept in the corner with my face turned toward the wall when she looked at me. I couldn't bear to look into her eyes . . . at her expressions of pain and anger. When my mom and I got home, I told her I wanted an abortion. She didn't respond nor did she object.

Yet, it was how the trauma of abortion showed up in my life that affected me the most. For weeks after the abortion, I sobbed and mourned most often when I was left alone to my own thoughts. Nightmares about babies crying all around me interrupted my sleep often. I suffered alone, never telling anyone what I was experiencing. Although my mother knew what I'd done, we never talked about it. "I did it," were the few words that let her know I went through with it. I'm not sure if her disappointment was too great or whether she was embarrassed; I just know we never spoke about it until nearly 15 years later when she apologized for not being there for me.

Between my extreme sadness, nightmares, and feelings of guilt, it's a wonder I managed to complete my sophomore year of college. Over time, I began to start feeling like myself again. By then, I'd broken things off with my boyfriend and did my best to move past the abortion, internal struggles, and shame that didn't leave me for years. So, I focused my attention on my studies, part-time work, and dating as if nothing happened.

I felt like I'd moved forward, until trauma showed up in my dreams on occasion or when I visualized the contents of that suction machine two, three, and even five years later. I wasn't okay because I had unresolved issues that required attention. I'd sit wondering if I would've had a boy or a girl and calculate my child's age on occasion. I wasn't okay when I was lying in that recovery room at 18, and I wasn't okay at 25, 26, or 28 when I was convinced I was ready to be married. Trauma spoke and added to the negative thoughts I replayed in my mind. *God is punishing you for what you did. You'll never have children. No man will want you after what you did.* I never spoke to anyone about what I'd experienced because I didn't feel like I had anyone to turn to during that time. I'd disappointed my mother, and I was ashamed to talk to anyone else. Trauma showed up and spoke to me in my dreams and negative thoughts I had about myself. Most of all, it showed up as shame.

I know that we live in a pro-choice era, but I can't help but wonder how many women made the choice and live with the trauma of abortion in ways that I did. Centers for Disease Control and Prevention's (CDC) reproductive health data says, "In 2016, 623,471 legal induced abortions were reported to CDC from 48 reporting areas. The abortion rate for 2016 was 11.6 abortions per 1,000 women aged 15–44 years, and the abortion ratio was 186 abortions per 1,000 live births." Of those women, past and present, I can't help but think about how informed they were about their choice and how that decision would impact their lives for years to come, in ways known and unknown. How many teenage girls and adult women alike suffered due to lack of information and education about how the choice would affect them physically and emotionally? The pro-choice voice is loud in our society, but I don't hear the concerned voices about women making an educated choice. I haven't heard the bullhorn or outcry shouting about the resources for women post-abortion. Where's the legislation mandating a series of counseling sessions for women? Where's the protest supporting an educated choice?

In 2019, debates about abortion were even louder. A number of states passed legislation, either further restricting or expanding abortion laws. For me, the larger issue is identifying political voices and thought leaders who are advocating for additional support for women who suffer post-abortion, no matter the gestational period. Women need to know the side effects of abortion that can cause challenges mentally, physically, and emotionally. I know I'm not the only one who has suffered in this way. The residual effects of abortion showed up in my life in ways I don't think

I can even totally describe. All I know is I wasn't okay, and at the time, I didn't realize that it was okay not to be.

Them

It seems like the world has a lot to say about singleness and why women struggle with meeting someone compatible enough to marry. This person and that person have great advice about how to find and keep a man. I've heard it all. Some things I put in my personal parking lot to consider later and other things were just plain old lies that I dismissed. Though not a comprehensive list, here goes, in no particular order:

- **You're just too picky when it comes to men.** I don't believe I'm picky. I just know my deal-breakers. But, if expecting a man to have basic positive attributes like respect, honesty, personal goals, and some ambition is picky, well, I guess, in that case, I'm picky.

- **He's the best you can do. Just marry him. He's a good catch.** This lie screams *settle and take what you can get.* My heart, spirit, and mind wouldn't allow me to settle for less than God's best for me. Should I have moved forward with the man who disparaged me just because he had a good job or was active in his church? Should I have moved forward or waited for the man who lacked confidence in himself and needed to work through his issues? I couldn't. I just couldn't.

- **You need a man to take care of you.** I've been an independent thinker and a self-starter for as long as I can remember. There was nothing included in any of my life plans that didn't involve hard work, and neither did it include being dependent on a man for financial support. My hope for a relationship was to be with a man who considers me his partner. I desired someone who understands what it means to build a life together, while sharing the responsibilities of the household.

- **All successful, educated, professional women marry later in life or not at all.** Although married women leaders were doing big things when I was growing up, I don't remember them being apparent to me. Now, I'm inspired by successful women who are married and still manage to pursue their careers. I look to Debbie Allen, First Lady Michelle Obama, Melissa Harris-Perry, Sunny Hostin, Tamera Mowry-Housley, or Congresswoman Ayanna Pressley as models for how to navigate a career and marriage. I also have the opportunity to look at married friends and married female mentors who've been able to sustain longevity in marriage and successful careers.

- **All your girlfriends are getting married, so you must be next.** I was the one single friend who was the last to get married among my circle of friends. Everyone around me seemed to focus on me being the unmarried one. Just because all my friends were engaged or married didn't mean I was next. I had to accept that even though I couldn't dodge the "Girl, you must be next" conversations.

- **Black women can't get a man because they are too aggressive and controlling.** The first time I discussed black women as aggressive was in my undergraduate African-American Literature course. We'd read and talked about black female stereotypes and their influence on the thoughts, opinions, and beliefs of people in society. This course is the reason I'm intrigued by the study of women and issues that concern them.

The next time I heard black women described as aggressive and controlling was from black men who were talking about how black women try to be the man in the relationship. I watched my stepfather and mother argue a lot. In the heat of the moment, he'd call her controlling. Looking back, I see why she felt like she had to take the lead in the relationship. He either wouldn't address household concerns at all, or he'd let her handle things he didn't seem to know how. I watched my mother get to the place where she'd just handle our household needs on her own without question. To me, she, like most black women, was doing what she felt she had to do to maintain the household.

The first time I can acknowledge being called aggressive was at work by a white female peer. We'd just started working together, and I had a presentation to give. After the meeting, she remarked that I was speaking aggressively during the presentation. I was confused. I'd given hundreds of presentations throughout my career and had never heard any of them described quite that way. Later, I spoke to her about her choice of words, and she explained that she meant I seemed confident when speaking. I thanked her for clarifying her comment, but I also helped her understand how I could've misinterpreted her remark. We walked away from that conversation with a clear understanding of how word choice is important and continued to work together to ensure we were understanding each other.

To my knowledge, I've never been called aggressive by a man. I've been called too ambitious but not aggressive. I can't imagine how being called too aggressive by a man would have impacted me. I just think aggressive is such a strong word, especially when used to define women. When my coworker called me aggressive, it felt like she was defining me as hostile or threatening, a total misrepresentation. For me, too ambitious felt like I was flawed. Either way, the labels stung me, and I didn't feel seen or understood for who I was by either of them.

- **There are not enough "good" men for all the "good" women in the world.** I heard this a lot from other women. While I did have some encounters with heartbreak, I met some pretty decent men through my travels, networking, and dating life. While those men weren't my Prince Charming, they were likely someone else's. Those encounters required that I get out of my comfort zone and travel beyond my community of friends and frequent hangout spots. I know good men are out there. For me, meeting them required that I try new things and experiences outside of my normal day-to-day activities.

- **Buying a house is a bad idea when you are a single woman.** I have no idea why some guys asked me, "What can I give if you have it all?" I never understood why they seemed to believe that material things were what I needed. I just can't put my finger on that one, but I do know that relationships with those men never materialized into anything. On the flip side, I've met men who weren't concerned at all about my possessions or accomplishments; they wanted to get to know me. When I met those types, I knew that there was a possibility to meet someone confident enough within himself to get to know me for me.

- **There is an expiration date on childbearing. You need to find a man now.** I can't count the unsolicited comments I've received about how old I was without children. What those people didn't know was I was already struggling with the trauma of abortion in ways that caused me to wonder if I'd ever be gifted with another child. To add, in my thirties, I began to deal with the rapid growth of fibroids that began to distort my uterus. Between managing my emotions post-abortion and facing the painful effects of fibroids, I became fearful about the possibility of not having a baby. Though I never felt like people were commenting about my status with malicious intent, I could never offer a response or rebuttal that made sense at the moment . . . only a meek smile and shrug. While I never believed in childbearing expiration dates, I was so consumed by my issues that I didn't have time to think about there being a due date for having a baby.

- **If you don't get married by 40, forget it.** I nearly believed this until I was 35 and unmarried. Although I'd heard this more than I can count, it's not true. I've met many women who married for the first time in their forties. In my twenties, it was hard for me to think about getting married anywhere near 40. But now, I believe love is timeless.

- **It's harder for a woman with children to get a man.** When my mother met my stepfather, I was five years old. He accepted me as his daughter without a second thought, and for that, I'm grateful. He never missed a birthday, special occasion, or a moment to share his wisdom with me. I'm forever thankful for his love. Men can love and care for children who aren't biologically theirs. I'm the product of a bonus dad.

- **You have to have sex with him in order for him to marry you.** In my late twenties, I made up my mind that I no longer wanted to have sex outside of the covenant of marriage. I felt like the temporary feel-good of sex was connected to my greatest emotional trauma and hurt. Even though I'd met men who tried to convince me that sex was necessary for the growth and deep connection of a relationship, my mind was made up (despite many temptations). But my decision not to have sex before marriage was a deal-breaker for them. Although my decision made dating complicated and sometimes impossible, my commitment to waiting for marriage was honored and reciprocated when I met my husband. He happened to be the one who initiated the discussion about waiting, and I was intrigued and relieved all at once during the getting-to-know-you phase.

- **All men cheat, get used to it.** I don't know if any of my boyfriends ever cheated on me and don't think knowing would add value to my life at this point. However, I do have a quiet hope in the integrity of men and believe that some men have enough self-control to resist temptation. I choose not to accept a sweeping generalization that lumps all men into such a category, particularly because I wouldn't want to be grouped among other women in a similar way.

- **Living together before marriage is a must.** I know many people believe that living together is non-negotiable before marriage. I never believed in that idea, nor did I ever do it. I felt it would confuse things for me emotionally; it also went against my belief system. To add, I've known people who lived together for years and separated not long after getting married. I've also known those who moved in together after they got married, and their marriage is still thriving. So, I don't believe living together before marriage offers any guarantees for a successful relationship.

- **When he left, he said, "I'm the best man you'll ever be with."** I think these words hurt me just as much as any breakup I'd experienced, and I almost believed him, until I remembered my value and what I brought to the table. I almost believed him, until I remembered that a man who would say something so demeaning and hurtful to me wasn't worth my time.

- **Not all women who desire marriage will get married.** Every time I heard this statement, it left me questioning myself and my desire for marriage, especially because I believed that God gave me the desire. For as long as I can remember, I heard people quote scripture about God giving believers the desires of their hearts. The part I missed in Bible class was the first part of the scripture, "Take delight in the Lord, and he will give you your heart's desires" (Psalms 37:4). I'm not sure if the women I heard say, "Not all women who desire marriage will get married" were referring to this scripture or not. I do know that I felt anxiety creep into my heart rhythm whenever I heard it. What I didn't understand at the time was that I had an active role to play if I hoped to receive any of my desires, hopes, or dreams. No matter the desire, my goals should always point me back to finding happiness in building a relationship with Christ.

It was me, it, and them that I almost let derail my ability to reach my full potential in life. But, if I wanted a relationship of any kind, I couldn't hold a mirror up to someone else's relationship or belief system. I'm convinced that everything that worked for them wouldn't work for me. If I'd let outside influences overload my thoughts, I don't think I would've survived singleness. I was already dealing with my internal thoughts and unresolved trauma. If I had any hope for transforming my life, it depended on denouncing lies and combating negative thoughts with positivity and affirmations. My survival hinged on changing my mindset.

What if I'd believed those who told me that all men cheat? How could I ever attract a man who doesn't subscribe to cheating? What I know for sure is constantly feeding myself negative thoughts never served me well. I know because I lived in the land of negativity too long. My negative thoughts attracted everything I never wanted—broken men, rejection, and heartbreak. Once I owned who I was with honesty, it was my responsibility to do something about it. Realistically, how could I have gotten into a healthy relationship during this time in my life? If I'd met the man of my dreams at, say, 25 while grabbing a cup of tea before work, would all that complicated stuff in me have translated well in a relationship? If, in that relationship, we reached the point of commitment, would the relationship have even worked with unresolved pain still haunting my dreams and suppressed in my memories? Probably not . . . but I can confirm that the relationship that began with a cup of tea didn't work out, not only because of me but because I'd attracted a version of me that wasn't ready either.

Readiness is a simple but important concept when thinking about marriage. Though I quoted Proverbs 18:22, "The man who finds a wife finds a treasure, and he receives favor from the Lord," I wasn't ready to be found. I was nowhere near the person I am today. It took me years to achieve the readiness I felt was necessary to even think about marriage. For that reason, I was surviving singleness in ways that didn't put me on the path I needed to thrive in singleness. It wasn't until I began to live my life on purpose in pursuit of my God-given destiny and purpose, that I was able to see a shift in my life. I had to learn how to manage my heart rhythm before considering a relationship. For me, surviving singleness involved acknowledgment and self-reflection. I had to do the pre-work for my healing before I allowed someone else and all their complicated stuff to be a part of my life. It involved telling myself the truth and knowing the difference between fact and fiction. It involved finding the courage to let my journey be mine and mine alone.

TWO

Oh Where, Oh Where Is Boaz?

<hr>

Does that one true love even exist? The concept of finding "the One" is such a complicated topic.

I have no idea when I started hearing my friends ask, "Where's my Boaz?" with the most gleeful but serious tones. This question would most assuredly be followed by the most girlish giggles and amused response: "Girlllll, I don't know. Where's mine?" It was almost as if we were expecting an answer. I'd simply laugh and wonder, *Who knows?* Given my age, all I know is "Where's my Boaz?" has been a cliché since at least the early 2000s. There are whole books, podcasts, and women's faith-based workshops and conferences about Boaz and where and how to find him. I often chuckle about the social media posts I see about this topic. The posts remind me of the time when my friends and

I laughed, asking the question ourselves about Boaz. So, I can understand the premise, intent, and sincerity behind the question that's been posed by many women for years. Like, women literally want to know where their Boaz is, and I was no different at one time. But honestly, I'm sick of people saying it. Yeah, I said it. I think the concept confused me and helped cause me too much anxiety about marriage, especially in my twenties—leading to one of the causes of my elevated heart rhythm. Although I think society is getting there with this push toward women's entrepreneurship and freedom of choice to marry or not, we aren't there yet. I believe I managed my desire for marriage better during my singleness when I redirected my focus away from the mysterious Boaz ideal and toward purposeful living. I gravitated to the story about Ruth and Boaz in the wrong way. I was looking and asking God for my Boaz when I was really looking for representation and a model for seeking a Godly relationship.

The biblical story of Naomi, Ruth, and Boaz, is found in the Book of Ruth. Their story is packed with so many positive themes beyond the fact that Ruth and Boaz end up marrying in the end. For me, it's an encouraging story about faith, restoration, and redemption, while also an active demonstration of God's power, grace, and mercy in the face of such devastating circumstances. The Book of Ruth focuses on Ruth and Orpah, two women of Moab who had married two sons of Elimelech and Naomi, Judeans who had settled in Moab to escape a famine in Judah. Despite their efforts to flee from famine in another land, the husbands of all three women die. To survive, Naomi plans to return to her native Bethlehem and urges her daughters-in-law to return to their families. Orpah returns to her family, but Ruth refuses to leave Naomi and declares with much devotion, "'. . . Don't force me to leave you; don't make me go home. Where you go, I go; and where you live, I'll live. Your people are my people, your God is my god; where you die, I'll die, and that's where I'll be buried, so help me God—not even death itself is going to come between us!'" (Ruth 1:16–17 [MSG]). Ruth accompanies Naomi to Bethlehem. While there, Naomi is still mourning her loss, and Ruth finds herself gleaning in the barley fields. However, Ruth happens upon a prominent landowner named Boaz, who is also a distant relative of her late father-in-law, Elimelech. After Boaz observes Ruth and notices that she is new to the land, he offers Ruth special gleaning privileges and asks his workman to be kind to her. Once Naomi learns that Boaz has an affinity for Ruth, she knows that Boaz has a duty to take her and Ruth into his care because he is her near kinsman or a family member to her late husband—Elimelech. So, Naomi lays out a plan with instructions for Ruth. She advises Ruth to request that Boaz become her kinsman redeemer, a male relative who had the responsibility to act on behalf of a relative who was in trouble, danger, or need. Ruth carries out the plan and later marries Boaz. They would go on to become the great-grandparents of King David.

Although the question, "Where's my Boaz?" is now a cliché to me, the story of Ruth and Boaz is still relevant. Their story should continue to be discussed from all vantage points, even from the perspective of marriage and relation-ships. There is something to be said about following the instructions sent by God, which often leads to discovering purpose and destiny in such a unique and authentic manner. Ruth and Boaz's story also points women toward a relation-ship model . . . something many women have lacked for var-ious reasons. Their story also gives women a sense of hope. For me, Ruth and Boaz's story is less about them meeting and marrying than it is about the pathway that leads them to one another. This concept of pathways and preparation is so interesting to me because when my friends and I laughed all those years ago while asking, "Where's my Boaz?" we were definitely not concerned about the steps needed to prepare for our intended mate. While I can only speak for myself, I believe that none of us in our early twenties were thinking about pathways and preparation for marriage.

Ruth's story is so interesting to me from the perspective of marriage but also from the perspective of her personal development. While there are several things that led to her marriage to Boaz, I'd like first to acknowledge that she is a widow who was able to begin again. I can't imagine losing two loved ones in the way that Ruth does. She loses not only her husband but also her father-in-law under tragic circumstances. I'm certain that her life rhythm was inter-rupted by many days of grief and sadness that compromised her heart rhythm in ways that left her emotions unsettled. I can't imagine an emotional heart rhythm that's filled with that much grief. For me, Ruth finds the steadiness of her heart rhythm in her love and devotion to Naomi. With a simple act of commitment, I believe she finds a new purpose that resides outside of marriage; she becomes dedicated to love through service and care for Naomi. This idea about love is awakening in some regards because I see my story parallel with Ruth's story. It wasn't Boaz who offered her a new chapter in her life, it was finding a purpose that was grounded in love and devotion that shifted the direction of her life.

I also recognize that her second marriage to Boaz would perhaps not have happened without the first. Both marriages offered Ruth positive purpose and outcomes within her life, and from my perspective, both were a part of God's plan for her life. Ruth's decision to follow and heed Naomi's instructions regarding Boaz secured her future for the better in Bethlehem. There are so many what-ifs that come to my mind when thinking about Ruth's story and ultimate end. *What if Ruth had never married Naomi's son? What if Ruth returned to her family, instead of following Naomi? What if Ruth ignored Naomi's instructions?* Of everything that comes to mind, it is her persistent devotion to Naomi and willingness to follow her instructions that yield her a positive outcome. Ruth is also found and recognized by Boaz because of her work ethic. She was in the field working and minding her business with her focus on her purpose.

The Once Upon a Time Syndrome

As I reflect on my journey, early on, I believe my downfall was the idea of finding "the One" and this hard and fast belief in fairytale endings, which some call the Cinderella Complex. Colette Dowling explains the concept in *The Cinderella Complex: Women's Hidden Fear of Independence.* In it, Dowling says that women who embody the Cinderella Complex have a desire to be saved and taken care of by men, despite having their own goals and interests. And, in some cases, women give up their dreams and aspirations for the sake of men. From my perspective, I was raised to have a vision, goals, and dreams for my life. Yet, somewhere embedded in my psyche was an underlying desire to be saved by Prince Charming. I thought a man would fill the void left by my father, give me a sense of safety and protection, and validate my beauty. When I was growing up, most girls in my community were raised reading the stories about *Cinderella, Snow White and the Seven Dwarfs,* or *Sleeping Beauty.* While these stories have different plots, they have a few things in common. The princess is portrayed as the damsel in distress. Although she is self-sufficient, the overwhelming theme is the princess being saved from evil by Prince Charming.

It didn't help that the images I saw on television projected this idea that women and girls should patiently wait for Prince Charming to come along or weave the necessity for dating or marrying into many of the female characters' storylines. I absolutely loved sitcoms growing up in the '80s and '90s, and some of my favorite female characters' storylines likely left an impression on me. I so loved Whitley Marion Gilbert (Jasmine Guy) in the hit show *A Different World* (1987). As a spinoff from *The Cosby Show* (1984), *A Different World* hit primetime television during a time when young black youth needed inspiration and consistent, positive images on television. For some, the show offered the first introduction to college life from the black perspective. For me, Whitley was a well-off southern belle who was both sheltered and bougie. She was also one of my favorite characters on the show. Although viewers watched her evolve, when we first meet her, her elitist attitude, coupled with her struggles for acceptance by her mother, are of paramount importance to her character development. Whitley's mother, Marion Gilbert (Diahann Carroll), is a representation of her time. She portrayed the essence of a time when mothers pushed their daughters to get an education, while also urging them to make finding a husband a priority in order to secure their futures.

We see Whitley grappling with challenges and seizing opportunities to overcome her mother's expectations. Whitley toils with her mother's urgings to marry post-college graduation. However, we do see Whitley's growth from this bougie princess to a more well-rounded woman who is a little less self-absorbed and judgmental. A woman who, despite her mother's wishes, advocates for her career goals and marries the man of her choice, though not without warring within herself to make her own decisions, which is a departure from the way she was raised. In my eyes, Whitley's character isn't entirely fictional or isolated. Her storyline is one of many real-life women who struggle against the societal, familial, or personal pressures to be married within a prescribed timeframe. Whitley's storyline is also mine, except my mother didn't pressure me; I pressured myself and felt pressure from those around me. I set a timer for marriage. When that didn't happen, I was disappointed.

I can remember when many of my childhood friends were getting married when I was in graduate school. I was super excited for them and was even in a couple of weddings. Around that time, a woman who watched me grow up came up to me with a concerned look on her face and asked, as she grabbed my hand and stroked the top of it delicately, "Don't you want to get married? You are such a beautiful girl."

"Yes," I said as I pulled my hand back.

I've always remembered that interaction. I think it did something to my consciousness. I walked away feeling like something was wrong with me. I walked away feeling anxious about marriage. I walked away not feeling supported by the community around me. I walked away and never forgot because I was hurt; it was a sensitive topic for me. While I do believe she was genuine, why had this woman who interacted with me often never questioned me really about anything else? She never asked me about school, my aspirations in life . . . nothing. Why was she so deeply concerned about me getting married, as if I were someone with no other needs in my future? Why didn't she see that I was already putting enough pressure on myself and didn't need her adding to it? I was never able to answer my internal conundrum of why this or that; I will never know. But, I forgave her over time for the way the encounter made me feel. I forgave her because she was likely living with the Cinderella Complex just like I was.

The '90s didn't disappoint either. Hit shows like *Martin*

(1992) starring Martin Lawrence and Tisha Campbell and *Living Single* (1993) starring Queen Latifah, Kim Cole, and Ericka Alexander were incredible comedic sitcoms that offered viewers different perspectives on doing life with friends. At the core of each of their multi-layered plots was this concept centered on observing young black friends pursue their career goals, while also dating and living life with support from one another. They illustrate the synergy that's prevalent within the black community when togetherness and supportiveness are honored and respected.

Of particular interest to me are Gina Waters (Tisha Campbell) and Pamela "Pam" James (Tichina Arnold) in *Martin*, along with aspects of the relationship among the female characters in *Living Single*. Gina and Pam's relationship is a pretty typical example of how African-American girlfriends interact with one another. They are best friends who happened to work together. Gina is a successful marketing executive, and Pam is a member of the company's staff, who works closely with Gina on various projects.

In general, Gina and Pam have a great relationship. We see them have lots of fun and display much support for each other's personal and professional endeavors. Of the two, Gina is the one in a committed relationship with her co-star Martin Payne (Martin Lawrence), and Pam is single and active on the Detroit, Michigan dating scene. Gina's relationship with Martin is generally solid. They have their typical relationship arguments but work through them pretty successfully. Gina and Martin eventually marry, leaving Pam the only single female character on the show.

Although the interactions between Pam and Martin are funny and comedic lines are still quoted to date, Pam takes a lot of flak from Martin for being single. Pam never marries for love during the show's run. She comes close to marrying a wealthy older man, but that doesn't work out. Later, she marries a man for money and to help him gain his citizenship. The marriage was annulled once he was able to honestly prove his citizenship. I believe viewers are hopeful when she starts dating Martin's best friend, Tommy Strawn (Thomas Ford), but we never see them get to the point of marriage. However, we do see Pam happy with Tommy, leaving us on the edge of our seats regarding their possibility.

Pam's character is a representation of many women. She is beautiful, talented, career and goal-oriented, and single, although she has some "almost moments" that we don't see materialize into marriage despite her desire. With all this, I will say that we don't see Pam openly pine over marriage. We see her almost marry a man old enough to be her father, actively dating, and eventually falling for the man right under her nose. Her desire is prevalent, but for me, she is not portrayed as desperate. At the time, I wanted Pam to end up with Tommy . . . for them to marry and have children. I wanted that for her.

Whether Pam and Tommy's relationship would've evolved into marriage if the show had continued, I don't know. I do, however, have a few observations. Pam was progressive, and while her biological clock was acknowledged on the show, she was also focused on her career and being a supportive friend to Gina. We don't see Pam hell-bent on getting married, although there are instances where she expresses her desire for marriage. We don't even see Pam pressuring Tommy into marriage, which I can appreciate. I'm reminded of Amen (1986), an '80s sitcom, where Thelma Frye (Anna Maria Horsford) desperately seeks Reverend Reuben Gregory (Clifton Davis) to no end until he marries her. I appreciate Pam's ability not to be overcome by elements of the Cinderella Complex in ways that cause her identity to be subsumed by concepts and thoughts about marriage.

I view Pam in many respects as someone who was trying to find her way when it came to romantic relationships. Throughout the show's run, she dated different types of men. Their ages, economic statuses, and personality types ranged. To me, she was open to accepting love however it came to her. I don't have any conclusions regarding Pam's dating life and her willingness to date men at all ages and stages in life. I do know that I identify with her. I was open to dating different types of men too. Yet, I was searching for something in relationships and didn't know or understand what it was or looked like for me. I lacked male representation that offered me a model for which to start understanding my desires and shaping my standards and expectations for and in a relationship.

Living Single aired in 1993 and ended in 1998, just before I started college as a freshman at Morgan State University in the Fall of 1998. This sister circle of girlfriends had all the flare and jazz of fly girls in the '90s. Khadijah James (Queen Latifah) owned a monthly issued magazine called *Flavor*. She was dedicated to her business but was also open to meeting Mr. Right. Synclaire James (Kim Coles) was a receptionist at *Flavor* and aspiring actress who eventually married Overton Wakefield Jones (John Henton). Regina "Régine" Hunter (Kim Fields) was a boutique buyer and serial dater who was in search of an affluent husband. Maxine "Max" Shaw (Erika Alexander) was an accomplished attorney who didn't hide her sexual freedom. These girlfriends were also roommates, excluding Max (who lived in a brownstone just across the street). They experienced life together in New York City and supported each other through ups and downs of life, career, and relationships. They made me laugh, cry, and cheer them on as I watched their on-screen lives unfold. Though different storylines, each of the ladies in this circle of friends is in search of male companionship, perhaps for different reasons and with varying approaches. While I don't identify with one specific character on this show, I do see elements of the Cinderella Complex rising to the forefront of many of the episodes. While these women were independent, goal-oriented, and self-sufficient, each of their storylines in some ways revolves around the male characters filling a void, rather than adding to their already complete lives. Though I'm sure this is by design, I believe it continues to drive a narrative that doesn't serve women well in the long run.

Life's No Fairytale

It's with the background of childhood fairytales, and sitcoms of the '80s and '90s that I entered my black college experience, active dating, and relationships. With the hope of finding my Boaz somewhere between college graduation and graduate school, I also took with me no model beyond my idealistic thoughts about a fairytale ending for my life. Sure, I was full of huge dreams and had a strong family support system, but I can't put my finger on why I was left to figure out male-female relationships on my own. While I was independent and mature as a teenager, I still needed "the talk" about the birds and the bees. I needed a real discussion about men. I don't blame my mom because she probably never had the talk. She talked to me about God but never about men and relationships. She gave me all she had to help me survive, a push toward education, and a foundation in God. I believe she viewed me as an independent child who she didn't have to worry about because I'm the oldest of four and needed little instruction. To add, my mother was a busy single mother. Her focus was likely on providing for me and my siblings, while relying on her faith in God to help *her* survive. Even though I did what I was supposed to do, I had questions that never got answered. Well, maybe my questions did get answered . . . the hard way.

Here I was preparing for everything else in life, but I hadn't realized that getting and being married would take my work and preparation. What I hadn't realized was that I also needed to prepare on the front end . . . before I got into a serious relationship that would lead to marriage. My early years were spent in school training and becoming qualified for my career aspirations. When I decided to purchase my first home, I formulated a plan. I checked my credit, worked toward getting rid of excess bills, saved money, and did a lot of research concerning first-time home buyer programs in my area. I prepared weeks in advance when I had a special event to attend with my girlfriends. *Hmmm, what should I wear? What's the best shoe to wear with that dress? What to do with my hair?* I was preparing before I went on my first job interview, contacted a real estate agent, or hit that party with my girls. Yet, preparing for marriage never crossed my mind and because of that I was nowhere near ready to be married in my twenties and likely my early thirties. Gary Chapman's *Things I Wish I'd Known Before We Got Married* explains that "Most people spend far more time in preparation for their vocation than they do in preparation for marriage. Therefore, it should not be surprising that they are more successful in their vocational pursuits than they are in reaching the goal of marital happiness." Preparing never crossed my mind. My desire to be married was greater than my desire to prepare for marriage. And so, I was unprepared and focused on speeding my way through college into my career, hoping that if I achieved success in those areas, my professional timeline would align with my timeline for marriage.

Part 2

PLOT TWIST

THREE

The Bottom Line

❤

Don't ignore the signs that will expose the heart and true identity of a man. — Guana E. Williams, Esq., Mom

The bottom line is men will treat you how you allow them to treat you. It was up to me to set my standards and be willing to walk away if those standards were not clearly met. Now, by no means am I an unreasonable person. As a caveat, I define unreasonable as holding someone accountable for standards, acts, and habits that I will never attain. For me, it was never my goal to change anyone. I was a handful on my own. I simply realized that every good conversation with a man or cool vibe I felt didn't necessarily mean that he was "the One" for me. In those instances, I truly believe that the platonic relationship is okay to embrace. Yes, he might be fine—*insert deep breath*—and embody all the physical attributes that make the heart skip a beat. But, if there is something holding him back from pursuing a relationship, I prefer to get a handle on my emotions before I fall too hard for someone who has placed me in the friend zone. I've never been too fond of wasting my time, so I learned to move on and accept a new friend without benefits or cut the tie.

As I matured, I began to view relationships like a business partnership with a few bonuses, probably because I operate best when things are organized and focused. I also realized that moving too fast into a relationship was an enemy to the balance of my heart rhythm. As with preparing to go into any business deal, there is a great deal of research conducted to learn more about each partner. Everything from assets, acquisitions, accounting, investors, and debt are discussed based on the provided supporting documentation. Many preliminary meetings take place to ensure that all parties are on the same page, seeking to achieve the same goal, bringing the same level of revenue, time, or energy to the table to help the business grow post-partnership. Like any business deal, one must be willing to walk away if it isn't agreeable to all parties, in advance of partnering.

But, like many women, I, too, have stayed too long hoping for a relationship to yield signs that the investment of my time and energy would lead to positive results and a future partnership. *I know I am not the only one.* I've heard several of my friends say they've stayed too long in relationships. I began to view relationships through the lens of a business owner seeking a partner—these types of relationships should typically be void of emotion. Business partnerships don't succumb to merely focusing on the outward-facing attributes of said partner's physical appearance. Likewise, when encountering men, I learned to set aside my emotions, physical attraction, and desire for a mate and focus on the hidden qualities that would serve me well in the long run. Let me be clear. This lesson didn't come without some hurt feelings or bad decisions. I earnestly sought to set aside my emotions and desires to see the heart of the man in front of me. And realistically, physical attributes of a man can fade. I wanted to get to know someone beyond his looks. *Who is he really? Even if he isn't where he wants to be financially or professionally, is he actively pursuing his dreams and vision for his life independent of a woman? What's his relationship with God like?* Based on my observations of other relationships and my own interactions with men, here are some things that I paid close attention to in addition to being prayerful about my relationships:

1. ***Relationship with Christ.*** I take my faith and relationship with Christ seriously. Likewise, I never dated a man who didn't express having a personal relationship with Christ. I specifically wanted my mate to not only have a relationship with Christ but also serve as an active member of his own church. *Why was this important to me?* I've always been an active member of a church and wanted to be with someone who enjoyed volunteering to do church work just as much as I did. My faith is a driving force in my life, and I desired a man who could be the spiritual leader of my household. I needed a man who could pray and hear God for direction for

our family. I needed a man who could serve as a trusted voice from God. I didn't want my mate to attend church just because I do. I wanted him to have an authentic relationship with Christ aside and apart from me.

2. ***Moral and Ethical Values.*** While moral and ethical values stem from a person's core beliefs and are often derived based on their environment, for me, certain human behaviors are off limits. Ethics are the codes of conduct by which society establishes its morals, right and wrong behavior. For example, ethics will prevent someone from acting upon the desire to run a red light while driving, which has been established by society as not only wrong but also breaking the law. Morals and ethics will cause one to choose the right path, even if the wrong path is more enticing. For me, an open display of a man's morals and ethics gets at the heart of his level of honesty and trustworthiness.

3. ***Passion and Clear Vision for the Future.*** Passion, coupled with hard work to produce and create the future desired, is one of the most attractive attributes that a man can possess in my book. A man who is actively pursuing his destiny, while also yielding results has my vote any day.

4. ***Good Decision Maker.*** The choices we make define our future. I could only weigh a person's decision-making skills based on where they have been and where I see them going. No, I haven't always made the best

decisions . . . no one has. However, it is so important to learn from mistakes, with the hope that one can avoid the same mistakes in the future. When dating, I used the getting-to-know-you phase as my opportunity to listen and observe. I paid attention to the stories about a man's past, observed the fruit of his decisions, and made mental notes about his current decision-making skills.

5. ***Financially Responsible.*** An ability to manage money and assets efficiently, with a particular interest in paying bills on time and maintaining a good credit score is more than a plus. It's a must.

6. ***Great Self-Esteem.*** A man who understood his value and self-worth, while also exhibiting great self-esteem and confidence piqued my interest. It was so important for me to connect with a man who understood that his value was not measured by material things, because I accomplished a lot at a young age. It concerned me when someone I was getting to know made comments or sly statements about me owning my own home or having two cars. It was a deal-breaker when they'd attempt to figure out how much money I made. Statements about my material possessions let me know that they were less concerned about my personality, goals, and life's vision and found my material successes problematic, whether consciously or unconsciously. I needed my man to be okay with me being a professional woman leader without being intimidated.

While the areas I listed are subjective, I can only measure the compatibility I have with another person based on whether I feel like I could live with what they are bringing to the table. For example, I could never be with a man who didn't have career goals or a job. I'm a hard worker at my core. For most of my life, I have had more than one stream of income. I could never be with a man who is not a hard worker. It just wouldn't work for me. Just like, I have recognized that I worked better with men who had a father or father figure in their lives.

My experience with men with daddy issues never worked. I needed a man who, at some point in his life, received some positive affirmation and reassurance about his manhood based on guidance from another man, whether by means of his father or male figure. I never had good experiences with men who had daddy issues. Perhaps it was because I was working through my own. So, I often remarked amongst my girlfriends that "I need a man with a daddy. Both of us can't have daddy issues, especially if he hasn't acknowledged or started working through his issues."

With the aforementioned in mind, I'd like to lay out several case studies drawn directly from my personal experience. As a child, I was always a person who wanted to narrow things down to the bottom line, which is one aspect of my personality that flowed nicely into my single life. For me, some things are plain black or white. Either it is or it isn't. It's the truth or it's a lie. It's right or it's wrong. Besides, the signs don't ever lie. While dating, I knew exactly what I wanted and how I wanted to be treated.

Blind Date Blues

My one and only blind date was memorable and not in a good way. It was far from the love connection that Lauren Speed and Cameron Hamilton experienced on the hit Netflix series *Love Is Blind*, where a group of singles date for three weeks without ever seeing each other. I can't recall the year, but I had to be in college because I was still driving my 1990 red Ford Probe, two-door stick shift. One of my girlfriends called and asked me if I wanted to go to the movies with this guy she'd known in her neighborhood. He had a friend who wanted to hang out too. I supposed the friend's friend was for me. Although I wasn't super eager to meet anyone special, I decided to tag along because I wasn't busy that night. From my impression, my friend and her neighbor were neighborhood friends who happened to talk that day and decided to catch a movie. Apparently, he had a friend of a friend who could get all four of us into the movie theatre for free.

I drove that night. I picked up my friend, and we headed over to the movie theatre. We met the guys at the theatre entrance. Just like my friend's neighbor said he would, he dapped up some dude, and we walked right into the theatre for free. I was so taken aback by my "date" that I don't even know what we went to the movies to see. I don't remember his name, and I wouldn't know him if I saw him on the street. I couldn't stop looking at his head. This dude had this Coolio (the rapper)-looking braid going on with his hair, except he didn't have several braids sticking up on his head. He had one single braid that started at the nape of his neck and spiraled around his head until the end of the braid reached the top of his head and stuck straight up in the air. One spiraling braid!

"What's going on with his hair," I whispered to my friend as we approached them in the theatre.

"Girl, I don't know. I never hang out with him. Let's just watch this movie and go home."

My first mistake was going into that movie theatre. There were hardly any seats, and I had to sit and watch that whole movie in a row with Coolio's look-alike and separated from my friend. Though I survived the movie, I couldn't tell you what it was about because I'd look at the screen and then glance to my left looking at his head. It was this back and forth look . . . screen, glance, screen, glance, screen, glance for at least 90 minutes. I know he saw me looking at him, but I couldn't help myself. I'd had enough and couldn't wait for that movie to end.

My second mistake was agreeing to grab dinner with those dudes. By the time my friend and I reached the restaurant where we'd agreed to meet the guys, they'd already grabbed a table and ordered drinks. Despite how weird I felt about how my "date" looked, we all exchanged a few laughs over dinner.

Before long, these dudes started dropping hints about leaving without paying the bill. We caught on fast and started pleading with them not to do that. I had about $30 cash and my friend didn't have any money; we were in college. Back then, dinner entrées didn't cost that much. So, I told them, "Look, I've got enough to cover our food. Y'all gotta pay for your own food. Please." My friend begged them to pay too; she kept asking her neighbor not to leave. They'd ordered Long Island iced teas and several other drinks I couldn't name, and we knew that bill was high. But, they laughed and joked as if they'd done it before.

By then, somehow the waitress caught on too. She kept coming over to the table asking if we were ready to pay. We brushed her off and kept telling her to come back in a minute. Then, we turned back to the guys to plead with them not to skip out on the bill to no avail. It all happened so fast. We were done asking them to pay. I got my cash out. My friend stood up and walked toward the door. Then, I stood up and threw my money on the table and began to walk toward the door. As I pushed the door open, those yahoos brushed past me, running out of the door. They were serious, and I instantly became extremely scared. Their running made me run. I ran to my car, unlocked the door (there was no door clicker to unlock the door back then on a 1990 Ford Probe), opened the door, and unlocked the passenger side door.

Before my friend could close the door, I had that stick shift in reverse, backing out of the parking space. I can still remember her leaning out of the door, trying to grab the door handle while I was backing up. From my rearview mirror, I could see the restaurant rent-a-cop standing on the curb shouting and pointing at the car the guys were driving. They left us and pulled off speeding out of the parking lot at no less than 90 miles an hour. Next thing I know mall security was chasing their car out of the parking lot. I don't believe they caught them, as fast as they were going. I was so nervous I was shaking. We drove home in silent disbelief. I drove across town, dropped her off, and got to my house in 25 minutes, which was how long it took us to get there from her house at the regular speed limit. When I got home, everyone in my house was asleep. I couldn't sleep and stared at the ceiling for hours wondering if I'd hear the police knocking on our front door. Thank God, they never came to my door. I hoped the cash I left was some consolation.

Bottom line: I was traumatized. The experience was so unbelievable. Months later, my friend and I were able to share a laugh about the situation but not at the time. Some might call me superficial for focusing so much on his hair, but I just couldn't get past it. Even though I don't remember him being a bad-looking guy, I wasn't interested in being seen in public with him. I was 19 . . . maybe it was my youth. What I do know is . . . blind dates weren't my thing after that experience. I'd need all the details upfront about his occupation, special interests, and background, including seeing a picture before I'd accept another one. To add, I learned a few things from that experience:

1. Carry cash on a first and even a second date.
2. Drive my own car on all first, second, and maybe even third dates.

3. Vet all dates with someone who knows them well, if possible—looks, character, financial state, at minimum.

Needless to say, that was my first and last blind date. No thanks.

Are You Crazy?

We met at the mall. I was in the food court, grabbing something to eat, and he doubled back to get my number. We chatted for a few moments, and I waited on his call. He called me that evening, and we had a decent conversation. He seemed cool, so we talked on the phone for about two weeks before we decided to go out. He was a musician. We bonded over music and talked about all the artists we liked. We met at Red Lobster on a Friday night. After we ordered, we had a pretty good conversation, laughed, and joked a lot. When our food came, we started eating, and then all of a sudden, he asked me to lean in so he could whisper something to me. I put my fork down. Curious, I leaned forward as close as I could, and he said, "You see that couple behind me?" I glanced past his shoulder to see who he was talking about. "They think they're better than us because they're eating shrimp and lobster." I sat back in my seat, staring at him, wondering if he was serious.

Then, I said, "We have shrimp on our plates. What are you talking about? Do you know them?"

He went on to explain that he didn't know them but

that he had to be careful where he goes because people always think they are better than him. He said he can't be around bougie people. He literally said, "That's why I don't come to Red Lobster." I sat there stunned for a moment. *Is he paranoid about a shrimp and lobster meal at Red Lobster? We aren't at a fine dining restaurant like Ruth's Chris Steak House or Capital Grille.* I had no idea why he'd think that the people at another table had a problem with him because they ordered shrimp and lobster. No clue other than this man was crazy, which made me nervous. It was all so confusing, and I decided to get out of that restaurant. Without changing my composure, when the waitress came, I asked for a to-go box, which let him know I was ready to go. He requested the check. *Good.* We packed up our food, and he walked me to my car. I thanked him for dinner and took the long way home, looking in my rearview mirror.

Bottom line: In the words of Maya Angelou, "When people show you who they are, believe them the first time." He was dead serious about a couple at another table looking down on him because of the meal they ordered. He was giving me signs of a mental problem. Whether my assessment was accurate or not, I had no plans on exploring. He called a few times, but I put him on the do-not-answer list in my phone without a second guess. I hope I was wrong for his own sake.

Guh, Chew with Your Mouth Closed

Is it just me or is expecting a grown man to chew with his mouth closed and not lick all ten fingers in public not too much to ask? He was nearly ten years older than me but didn't look it. I met a well-groomed, well-dressed, professional man who had a real relationship with God. He smelled good too. But, when I watched him eat, my stomach turned. We talked for a few months on the phone and only ate together once. After the first time, I declined other dinner offers. He chewed with his mouth open and talked with food in his mouth too. Food fell *out* of his mouth. He also licked his fingers . . . all ten. I couldn't sit across from the table and watch him eat. I just couldn't. He was nice, despite my personal challenge. It wasn't him; it was me.

Bottom line: I'm sorry. Some things are deal-breakers. I just didn't see myself having a conversation with him later on in a relationship like—"Babe, can you chew with your mouth closed? Can you stop licking your fingers when we eat in public?" It was obvious to me that he'd been eating that way all his life. More importantly, despite getting along well, I didn't feel a real connection enough to move forward in a relationship. Plus, I'd always been told that small pet peeves turn into big arguments in a marriage. After a few months, we just parted ways. I did, however, see him later when I was on a date with someone else. When he got a chance to speak to me alone, he questioned me, "Why are you with him? Who is this?" I just looked at him. He had his own date that night. I hadn't seen him in over a year. In the few months that we talked and the one time that we went to dinner, we hadn't even kissed. *Bye! Why and how are you jealous?*

Getting-to-Know-You Phase

We never got into a relationship. We parted ways at the getting-to-know-you phase. On the phone one day, in what I thought was a casual conversation, he said, "I can find any female like you. There're plenty of women out here with degrees, a good job, and a lot going for them." I was quiet for a moment. Then, I hung up the phone. I was young and in my twenties . . . sue me. Hanging up the phone was the only way I felt would demonstrate how angry and tired I was of him. He called me right back and a couple times thereafter; I never answered the phone. I decided to let him go find one of those women. Some may feel I was too harsh but that wasn't the first time he'd said something like that to me. Why was he so concerned with letting me know that he had other options? Although I never discussed my personal life in ways that gloated about my accomplishments, he always felt the need to make mention of them, in what I felt was a negative way, which bothered me.

Bottom line: I was never willing to allow someone to be condescending, discrediting, or belittling toward me in ways that could potentially cause me to question myself. I wasn't willing to allow anyone to unravel my confidence in such a way. I absolutely view any form of that type of behavior as verbal abuse, and I could not allow myself to continue any connection with someone who showed me any sign or form of abusive behavior.

Friend Zoned

We got along great, spent several birthdays together, developed a sincere, authentic friendship, despite our attraction to each other. He was my go-to phone call when something went wrong and I was his. He told me he loved me often, and I responded with the same sentiment. We were highly attracted to one another and almost had sex a few times. We talked about being in a relationship but never moved forward.

In a casual conversation one day, he said, "Jas, you're just too ambitious. That's not what I'm looking for." It hurt, but I heard him. I listened. I didn't respond with tears or questions, nor did I turn away from my aspirations. I just heard him because he'd laid out his intentions for and with me. We were friends.

Bottom line: He was a good catch but just not for me. I was in the friend zone, and that was okay. We remained close friends until we each met the ones who we'd eventually marry.

A Taste of His Own Medicine

He broke my little heart when he broke up with me. I was so hurt, complete with excessive tears, mid-day crying sessions in the bathroom at work, and heartache so deep that I could literally feel the pain of heartbreak. Despite how hurt I felt, I had enough conversations with male friends to know how I needed to operate after this breakup; I decided to flip the script. Typically, I was the girl who called and texted … wanting answers about why a guy stopped calling, especially after a breakup or after someone I liked simply cut me off. I was the girl who cried on the phone, asking why we couldn't be together after a breakup.

Nope, not this time. As much as I wanted to call him, I never called, texted, or emailed after we officially broke up. I gave him silence, until I decided to answer his call a year later. When I answered the phone, he barely gave me a chance to say, "Hello" before he said, "You never call me. I'm the only one reaching out. I really want to be friends." *Oh really?!* I said to myself.

"I hope you're well, but I have no reason to be friends with you. I've moved on with my life."

"But, I have learned so much from you. You can't say you got nothing out of the relationship. I have good relationships with all my exes."

"I'm just not interested in any kind of relationship with you."

Without much conversation after our exchange that day, we hung up the phone. We texted for a few months after, and I even met him for lunch a couple of times, but that was short-lived. I was done.

Bottom line: Although I had a few committed relationships, this relationship was different. He walked away from me without any warning. One day we were laughing and joking, and the next day he was gone . . . no call . . . no show . . . for more than a month. By the time I spoke to him after his disappearance, my emotions were all over the place. My confusion turned to worry about him and then to extreme anger. I felt like I deserved an explanation about his whereabouts, whether he was alive or dead or, at minimum, the decency of the "It's not you; it's me" conversation.

Finally, we had some vague discussion about how he was going through a lot and needed to be alone to work on himself. It was after his "explanation" for avoiding my calls that I was determined to give him a taste of his own medicine. When we officially parted ways, I was done, but I knew he'd be back because they always come back, according to the women in my family. In the end, I accepted what he wanted and moved on to focus on my healing. I wasn't willing to allow him to call, text me, or walk in and out of my life when he felt like being bothered. That relationship left me too hurt to even think of going back, though he had the audacity to ask me to wait for him, once we did speak after a year. He wanted me to wait until he got himself together, whatever that meant. Waiting for him was an unthinkable request and not worth it for me in the long run.

The relationship added no value to my life and wasn't worth the six months I spent in it. In hindsight, I often acknowledged that I wasn't happy being with him. I gave more than I received. I took on his burdens while forsaking my own. I continued even though all the signs were telling me to let it go. I was settling. Had I gotten stuck in a dead relationship, I don't know where I would be today.

The one thing these men had in common was that they were never really my type, even though I thought that at least two of them were. Like many women, I got so lost in saying, "my type." I thought I knew my type, even when I didn't know myself; my inner peace was compromised in every instance. I never felt like I was in a safe place while getting to know or dating them. I couldn't be myself. Sometimes I felt like I had to hide my relationship with God. At times, I dumbed myself down to make men feel comfortable in their skin. I questioned myself about whether I involved myself in the right relationship. This feeling in my belly caused me to feel anxious while dating or in a relationship. I had no peace.

Even though I didn't always get it right, the bottom line was each of these examples presented clear signs that a relationship would never work with or for me. My gut never lied to me. I've known when I was being lied to, and when I was led to believe that a relationship was possible when he truly had no intention toward me. I believe it's best to move on to maintain peace of mind and avoid settling for less, without letting my emotions and desire for a relationship mislead me into ignoring the signs. Like my mom always said, the signs never lie, listen to them.

FOUR

Moonlight Path

I think every girl in my high school wore the Bath & Body Works lotion and body spray collection Moonlight Path. It was all the hype. It seems like me and my friends went from wearing our mothers' perfume to wearing Moonlight Path overnight. I don't recall much from high school but I do know that I wasn't in the in-crowd, nor was I totally awkward. I liked the middle ground . . . the outskirts of both groups, where I was free to roam, observe, and be friends with whomever I wanted. I didn't hate high school, and I didn't love it, which is why I accepted the offer to finish school a year early. It was, however, the first time I recall trying to understand who I was, and that was tough.

I struggled with finding confidence with my looks and my body type amongst girls who had blossomed earlier than I did. I questioned myself about how I wanted to dress. Was I the girl who wore skirts and heels, or was I the tight jeans and high-top Reeboks girl? I opted for the Xscape or TLC girl group-look of the '90s.

High school also came with the possibility of dating boys and thoughts about those boys not wanting to date me. Though I felt some boys were interested, I was only asked out once, and that was to the senior prom. I had no idea he was interested. I shouldn't have declined. I went to the prom with someone I met from another school, but I think I would've had more fun with the boy from my school. He was a cool kid, and I observed him having a lot of fun that night. Among all the things that I recall from high school was the fear I had of the unknown. I was uncertain about who I was becoming. To add, graduating at 16 and going to college was scary and daunting all at once. At this moment, my heart rhythm felt steady but could've easily lost its beat.

Looking back, it's so interesting that the fragrance name Moonlight Path was indicative of what I understand about my life now. Fear of the unknown represented a darkness for me, in the midst of all the light illuminating from the celebratory moments of graduating and being accepted into college. This feeling of fear traveled with me into college and beyond, even though the moonlight consistently offered me glimpses of light. In my youth, I was too afraid of the dark to recognize the moonlight path.

Now, I'm not afraid of the dark anymore. Somewhere along life's moonlit path, I matured and accepted the goodness and Godness that heartbreak, hurt, and disappointment can offer. Now, I reverence the dark spaces in my life that brought on forms of overwhelming emotion, depression, and, in some instances, feelings of dread.

My father abandoned me when I was just about four years old and that was my first encounter with heartbreak. It was also the first time I felt like a man didn't want me and the onset of feelings of rejection. I loved my father and desired a relationship with him for many years after he left. As time progressed, I often forgot he existed and can literally count the times I saw him on one hand as a child—ages 7 and 16. Although I don't recall thinking much about him growing up, that didn't stop the residual effects of his absence from triggering my emotions after a breakup. Although I dated throughout college and into my twenties and thirties, I had about three serious boyfriends and two of those relationships resulted in my most devastating heartbreaks. There were tears for days, weeks, and even months. It was heartbreak from the ones I thought I loved that catapulted me into an overwhelming sense of fear about my future. Feelings of rejection and abandonment surfaced in ways known and unknown. Yes, those dark spaces and those that I don't care to mention are now like footprints in the sand—a fading memory.

Yet, even at my lowest points in life, I must acknowledge the glimmers of light that often gave me the strength to get up every day and try again. These were times of encouragement that gave me just cause for increased hope and peace while going through challenging circumstances. Sometimes right in the middle of a negative thought, there came a kind word from a stranger. *I don't know you well, but you add so much value to our meetings. You know you really look nice today.* As tears streamed down my face just before crying myself to sleep, there came a phone call from a friend that I hadn't heard from in a while. *Hey, Jas. I was thinking about you and decided to call you.* Consumed by heavy emotion with no view in sight for anything positive, I'd encounter a dynamic, life-changing sermon from one of my favorite preachers and feverishly take notes. I wrote snippets of my sermon notes on Post-its and placed them on my bedroom mirror or in my office workspace. *God has the final say. He has His hand on your life. He is the same God today, yesterday, and forever. You are more than your present circumstance. God loves you too much to let you miss it.* Although I overlooked these moments at the time, they were lighting my path toward a transformed mindset.

As I grew to understand myself, moonlight paths became more than a fragrance I wore in high school but rather a scientific concept that helped me make sense of my life. I like how *Science and Health* explains the phases of the moon and helps me further contemplate the glimpses of light along my life's path. This textbook lays out a basic explanation—

> The moon shines with reflected light . . . It borrows light from the sun . . . We see different parts of the lighted sides at different times. We may see all of the lighted side, part of it, or none at all. What we see depends upon the position of the moon in relation to the sun and the earth. (1993, 156)

Based on everything I can remember from high school science class, I can confirm that the moon isn't shining at night. From our perspective millions of miles away from the moon, it only looks like the moon is shining bright. It's reflecting light from the sun, which allows the moon to be illuminated at night. It's our perception. Moonlight simply means we are seeing the sun from a different position. How we view the moon and sun depends on the position of the earth as it rotates on its axis within a 24-hour period and orbits around the sun once within 365 days—hence the phrase, *a trip around the sun.*

Enough of all that science stuff. Here's what I've come to understand: In some regards, I believe light and darkness are synonymous. If I think about it from the perspective of the sun and moon, light and darkness are based on my perception of them. My perception of light and darkness was shaped in childhood. As a child, I was conditioned to believe that anything good dwells in the light, with color and brightness, and anything bad lives and lurks in the darkness. This concept led me to believe that light and darkness are different, leaving one to be embraced and the other to be feared.

What I now know is how this simple concept shaped my thinking about life. When difficult situations interrupted my life rhythm, the unknown outcome scared me. I wasn't patient enough to experience the situation from a place of positivity. Instead, I adopted a negative perception about the outcome of the situation and felt fear concerning a future that gave me no cause to fear it. When, in fact, darkness has just as much goodness to offer as the light. Even God views light and darkness, day and night as synonymous. Psalms 139 explains,

> Is there anyplace I can go to avoid your Spirit? to be out of your sight? If I climb to the sky, you're there! If I go underground, you're there! If I flew on morning's wings to the far western horizon, You'd find me in a minute—you're already there waiting! Then I said to myself, "Oh, he even sees me in the dark! At night I'm immersed in the light!" It's a fact: darkness isn't dark to you; night and day, darkness and light, they're all the same to you. (Psalms 139:7-12 [MSG])

Though I didn't understand it at the time, this passage serves a reminder that even when I'm experiencing my darkest moments the Lord is my moonlight. It reminds me that there is no place the Lord can't find me to be my comfort and my hope. He's there reflecting just enough light to guide my path because He is with me in the good times and the bad times.

Yet, before I had a chance to unpack my thoughts about light and darkness, when I found myself feeling down in life, my heart rhythm was affected, and I began to display symptoms of depression. All I wanted to do was be alone inside my bedroom in the dark with the door closed—left only to fester my fear and sadness. For days, I'd live in what

I felt was a dark cocoon. When I felt my best and thought all was well in my world, I felt like the sun was shining on me. I was eager to get out just to get some fresh air or do things like shopping and hanging out with family or friends. In either case, looking back, I had the wrong perception about my life and lived with a false sense of reality.

In my youth, too often, I reveled in the grandeur of what seemed to be sunny days when the real essence of what life had to offer me was cultivated in what I perceived to be dark nights. I was seemingly at my best when I felt everything was going well—dating, school, or work. Yet, when my life rhythm was interrupted by crises—disappointments or challenges at work—I spiraled downward off my high and felt I was living under a dark cloud. In those moments, my youthful mindset trapped negative thoughts that led no-where. *Life is over. You'll never find a good man. You're not that pretty. If you could just lose a little more weight. You're going to stay in this job forever. What if you don't this . . . And, what if you don't that . . .* When I think about all the negative thoughts I fed my soul, I quiver. When I think about how much time I wasted not affirming and building myself up with positive thoughts, I cringe.

With time, I learned to shift my perception when neg-ative thoughts try to consume me. I remind myself of how far I've come . . . that I did snap out of it and get myself together. I'm reminded of how much I grew and developed emotionally and spiritually because of those dark moments that I feared. I remember that what I see and understand about my life depends on the lens that I choose to view the situation through. Now, I know that the sun was shining bright during my dark moments because what appeared to be dark was reflecting light and teaching life lessons that could only be gleaned in dark spaces. Those challenging moments that seemed to overtake my life and thoughts were a part of my moonlit path toward my destiny and a bright future. Crises and chaos pointed me toward transformational opportunities to create, evolve, and reshape my life. I've heard countless stories about people who lost jobs and found greater opportunities waiting for them. There are thousands of women who suffer the loss of a marriage or children, and out of their pain comes a better mate or a life's purpose that brings them fulfillment. There are endless stories about crises and chaos shifting lives for the better.

> "Crises and chaos pointed me toward transformational opportunities to create, evolve, and reshape my life."

In those moments when I felt like the world was coming to an end, I had a choice. I could choose to dwell in the dark times or learn something about myself and my ability to adapt to the situation. Darkness taught me some of the greatest life lessons because there are always glimpses of light. It took the right perception for me to see what was there all along. How would I have known that I could survive loss if I never lost a love? How would I have known that I had surrogate fathers all around me, if I'd never felt fatherless? How would I have known that God mends broken hearts, if my heart was never broken? And, how would I have known that intentional focus on healing and wholeness would transform my identity? Crises and chaos are tools that can lead to creative transformation, personal growth, and development. I believe that sometimes God will allow crises and chaos so He can establish His plan.

Looking back, every moment I viewed with negativity thrust me closer to His ultimate plan and purpose for my life. In moments of darkness, it was often hard for me to find glimpses of light that were always there to either protect, transform, or comfort. In retrospect, the positive growth and development that I experienced when I thought I was surrounded by a cocoon of darkness were worth it all. So no, I'm not afraid of the dark anymore.

FIVE

A Scream Saved My Life

Promise me, O women of Jerusalem, not to awaken love until the right time. (Song of Solomon 8:4)

Severe heartbreak was the gateway to my identity transformation, and it was a loud, screeching scream that let me know I was ready to heal. There were times when hardships in life left me speechless. All I knew was this feeling of excruciating pain, with no bruises as proof of contact. I felt moments when life hits so hard that it feels like an unexpected gut punch from a heavyweight champion. Psychologists call those feelings emotional pain. In my quest to understand what I was feeling, I happened upon Alan Fogel, a professor of psychology emeritus at the University of Utah in Salt Lake City. His *Psychology Today* article explains that when people experience emotional pain, the same regions of the brain are activated as when physical pain is felt.

The difference is . . . medicine is not often the go-to aide for stopping or mitigating the challenges of emotional pain.

Fogel further says that "Emotional pain may be located in the body in those places where an expression was meant to happen but failed to materialize." In instances of neglect, Fogel also suggests that such emotion can manifest as neck pain. At the same time, rage and hatred can show up in our lives as physical gut pain in the form of constipation, nausea, or irritable bowel syndrome. Comparatively, the American Psychology Association says that the pain of heartbreak is similar to the pain of a broken arm.

I felt a deep connection to this concept when I read it. It helped me understand and confirm how emotional pain manifested as physical ailments in my body. I saw a trend. As a child around five or six years old, I can remember crying in my bedroom at bedtime. I'd been thinking about how much I missed my father for most of the day. There I lay in my bed in the dark with only a night light to shield me from the fright I felt in the darkness. Uncontrolled tears streamed down my face leaving my pillow to catch them. I cried because I wanted my father. I cried because I didn't think he wanted me. I cried. I cried and cried until I vomited. I thrust my body forward, hanging my head over the side of my bed, hoping to avoid soiling my bedding. It didn't work. I screamed for my mother, and she came running right away. As she flicked the light switch, she hollered, "Oh my goodness! What's wrong?"

"I threw up."

She picked me up out of bed and spent at least an hour

bathing me, cleaning the floor, and changing my sheets. By then, I was okay. She took my temperature only to find that I didn't have a fever. That night, I found peaceful sleep next to my mother.

Though I don't recall ever experiencing the manifestation of emotional pain in that way again, I can pinpoint a gripping experience with grief that left me literally voiceless. I'm the oldest of 14 grandchildren and shared a loving relationship with my grandmother. Years later, when I was 28, she passed away. I lost my voice for nearly three weeks after we buried her. My only form of communication was a faint whisper or handwritten notes on a notepad. I soon realized that the trauma of death affected me emotionally and physically. This incident caused me to recall other times where my emotions manifested as sickness.

With newfound insight about the influence of emotional pain in my body, I can look back on my experiences with heartbreak beyond the sadness and anger that accompanied it. For me, emotional pain surfaced through social rejection—purposeful exclusion from an individual or group. According to researchers, it can have a severe impact on one's emotional health. I've seen social rejection so apparent in schools when students are bullied and deliberately excluded from interacting with other students. I've observed it when a family member is estranged because of an unsettled dispute. Like many women, I've felt the pain of social rejection after a breakup. This concept exposes how emotional pain wars against the body, mind, and soul. I'm convinced that this type of pain caused my emotional instability.

Social rejection came to me first by means of parental abandonment. From there, a few encounters with heartbreak further exacerbated the emotional pain I felt. The rug was ripped from beneath me in my last relationship before I met my husband. That last time was the worst. He was the guy who I gave a taste of his own medicine when we broke up, despite feelings of rejection that left my heart feeling shattered with no hope for mending. I was depressed and lost ten pounds in a matter of a month. Tears consumed my mornings and evenings. I'd experienced a heartache that derailed my prescribed life's timeline, as I dealt with what I felt to be a physical pain that almost left me paralyzed. I was a mess. Couldn't eat. Couldn't breathe. Couldn't find my focus. Couldn't articulate myself. I was a functioning emotional wreck who worked, went to school, and returned to my cocoon to cry and sleep. I repeated that cycle for months, until I turned the corner with the help of my mother and faith in God.

Somehow, through all the tears, this experience with heartbreak awakened me to a higher consciousness and awareness about myself. It was the first time that I actually felt my emotional heart arrhythmia and the rapid cadence of my heartbeat that caused the anxiety and stress that led to depression. I'd experienced relationship heartbreak in the past but nothing like this. This time was different. Fogel says, "Feelings of insecurity get the heart and the breath out of sync[h] and activate the sympathetic nervous system as if we were dealing with a threat (elevated heart rate and blood pressure), and can create a sense of unease in the chest, and even pain." I felt every sense of unease that Fogel alluded to with this statement. I was nearing my deadline for marriage and thought that the last one was "the One." I became sick to the point of nausea. My chest felt like I'd had my ribs cracked open in preparation for heart surgery. Even without a medical examination, I can confirm that my heart was broken so much that I could feel my elevated heart rate consistently.

I'd reached my breaking point and was desperate for a change in my life. I clung to my mother, spiritual advisors, scripture reading, and positive affirmations to rejuvenate my mind and spirit. I turned inward to my faith and decided to give up control of my timeline. The trauma of that relationship breakup left my heart sorely sensitive, and honestly, I was sensitive even to touch. It hurt to breathe and speak. Coupling the pain and trauma of my past with one relationship disappointment and heartbreak after the next, I was a mess. Compounded crises left my mind in chaos and my heart sick. My heart had taken all it could, and I was overcome by hurt for several years after that relationship ended. I dated very little and felt like I needed to guard my heart with all earnestness.

I Wasn't Okay

Sometimes everything crumbles for a reason. Too often, I said I was okay when I wasn't. I was reckless. I'd jumped into that relationship too fast, and within a

> Sometimes everything crumbles for a reason.

few months, we were talking about getting married. He showed me many signs that he wasn't "the One" for me, but I continued. Though it hurt, the breakup was good for me because I needed to address the most complicated parts of my being. Once I started admitting that I wasn't okay and that I wasn't ready or capable of choosing the right man for myself through the lens I was looking, things got better. I made a decision to choose me over everything. In doing so, I was choosing to allow God to establish His plan. More importantly, I relinquished my control and submitted to His timeline, but that didn't come without a lot of soul work. Finding the right pace for my heart rhythm wasn't easy. It came with tears, mistakes, and some fears, but a more reasonable pace came with time, honesty, and forgiveness. It was an evolutionary process that took several years.

I began really wrong from the start of my healing journey. I began in tears and found myself back on the floor crying at my mother's house, even though I'd gotten up off that same floor years ago. Except this time, I wasn't 20; I was near 30, all grown up, with a great job, and living in my own home. Yet, there I was weeping again over being rejected by another man and with negative thoughts festering.

I remember the first time I gave voice to my tears. I sashayed into church on a sunny Saturday morning for a women's day event and took my seat. I'd just left the nail salon with a fresh mani and pedi and was feeling pretty good that day; I hadn't shed heartbreak tears in a few days. The day's speaker had traveled all the way from the Caribbean Islands, and I knew I was in for a day full of insight and encouragement. Nearly as soon as I sat down, she summoned me to the front of the church. I assumed she wanted to greet me before the event started.

Barely saying a word, she grabbed me, wrapped her arms around me, and hugged me so tight. It was as if she knew all the pain I'd experienced over the last several months. It was as if she saw into my soul and recognized that I was weak, even though I'd adorned myself outwardly. The more she tightened her grip around me the more my tears flowed. She held me for at least ten minutes before I let out this high-pitched scream that made those in the room stand still. I screamed at least five times. Each time I screamed, the octave went higher. Before I knew it, I felt the greatest sense of relief and weight lifted off me. That day, my scream spoke. It told my story. It spoke of the little girl who cried herself to sleep wishing her father was there, spoke of the trauma of abortion, and spoke of every disappointment and every let down. It spoke of my past and spoke of why I did what I did. It spoke of the essence of who I was and desired to be. Most of all, my scream let me know I was truly ready to heal.

Perfect Timing

It was nearly five years before I got into another relationship and the next one was with my now-husband. There's so much I could say about what I did with my time during the wait for who I'd been accustomed to calling "the One." I'll begin with my summation: I found a better version of me. Then, I'll offer the essence of my evolutionary process.

After I went through the typical rituals of heartbreak—incessant crying, questioning why me, and deep-seated sadness—I got myself together and turned back to my foundation and faith in Jesus Christ. Healing began with honest repentance and forgiveness. I prayed prayers of repentance about my past. Over time, I shifted to prayers of thanksgiving and petition about my present and future. As I prayed, my heart began to shift away from self-doubt, pity, sadness, anger, and fear toward gratefulness, thankfulness, and joy. I'd been in church all my life, but my earnest desire for a change caused me to delve deeper into the Bible for answers and strength. I'd known God through my mother. Through my own experience, I'd begun to really know God and His power for myself. Through my prayers and readings, I surrendered my will to God's plan for my life, even if that meant singleness for me, though a hard pill to swallow. Nearly every morning for years, I opened the Bible and really began to recognize the love of Jesus through its stories, life lessons, and strategies for living a Christ-centered life. I searched my Bible for scriptures about finding healing, refuge, strength, peace, and joy in God. Most mornings, I dedicated at least an hour to meditation, scripture reading, and prayer. Each week, I fasted from food and television at least one day. I began to see myself in the scriptures in ways that allowed me to apply the teachings of Jesus to my life. I used the Book of Psalms as affirmations and the Book of Proverbs as instructions for living.

For many years prior, my mother recommended that I read John and Paula Sandford's *Transformation of the Inner*

Man. This time, I took her advice and read it from cover to cover in a matter of a week. Then, I began to use it as a manual of sorts. In it, I was guided through the process of achieving true healing and wholeness. As I read, I was deeply touched by their words and found myself identifying with the content. At times, I paused to reflect on all aspects of my life. Other times, I was brought to tears because I saw where I'd errored.

One of the most impactful parts of the book was the chapter on forgiveness, "The Central Power and Necessity of Forgiveness." In reading it, I began a forgiveness journal that documented everything I needed to forgive myself for, while also listing things I wanted to forgive others for. It extended from trivial disagreements I'd had with friends, unspoken grudges against family members, pages dedicated to releasing hurt caused by my father, to tear-filled pages about ex-boyfriends, pre-marital sex, and my decision to have an abortion. Though it took me some time to reflect on all the things that I wanted to forgive, I began to verbally forgive in my bedroom. With two words, I said, "I forgive . . ." and began to recite aloud every subject that I felt needed audible acknowledgment . . . anything that stung my soul . . . anything that made me mad just at the mere thought . . . anything that caused tears to well up in my eyes. I forgave myself, people, places, things, and actions almost daily until I didn't feel the sting, anger, or tears. Even though some things took longer than others, I said, "I forgive . . ." until I believed it and it changed me over time.

Forgiveness liberates the soul. It removes fear.
That is why it is such a powerful weapon.
\- Nelson Mandela

Then, I had the courage to forgive my father and choose to move forward. I began in my journal, and that evolved into the hard conversations that were necessary for me, despite what I thought the reaction would be. By then, we were communicating after several years of not speaking; he had just gotten back from Sierra Leone after more than two years. He is a proud West African man who thought he could step back into my life on and off and be an authoritative father. Throughout my childhood, I only saw him just about three times. From there, it was almost as if he had the calendar marked for my high school and college graduations. He'd show up just in time to attend and hang around for several months. He'd call, check on me, and we'd even have dinner on occasion, hang out on Saturday mornings, or hit the occasional African party in D.C. I could even anticipate receiving the occasional Valentine's Day card when he was active in my life. *The first time I received a Valentine's Day card from him, it did so much for my heart rhythm. It was as if that small gesture filled a small measure of the void I felt for my father's love.* But, it wouldn't be long before I wouldn't see or hear from him for months and even years. He'd get fed up with the hustle and bustle of the States and emphatically say, "I'm going home." Home for him meant Freetown, Sierra Leone, to enjoy the Atlantic Ocean and as much jollof rice and fresh fish as he could take. Home didn't include me, and didn't include calling me. Though I'd gotten used to him leaving, there was still a void, a girlish desire for Daddy.

After his last extended stay home in 2011, he was back like clockwork about two years later. He called as per usual and said, "I'm back. Let's meet for lunch." By then, I'd settled in knowing that he could never be the father I'd imagined, and I'd done much of my soul work in my journal. This time, I was committed to having a hard conversation, and a 30-minute lunchtime wouldn't suffice. We met for dinner not far from my job. When I saw him, we embraced and he was noticeably not presenting as the boastful, strong-headed African man that I'd always known him to be. He was different. Perhaps that was by design from God.

Nearly as soon as we sat down, he began to tell me about his trip with so much joy in his disposition. It was like he knew I wanted to talk. Just as abruptly as he began recalling his travel log, he said, "I know I've been bad." With those words, I'd found my moment to get it all off my chest, for me, no matter the response. I talked for about 45 minutes, and he just listened. I began with— "I'm angry because you weren't there. I'm angry because you walked in and out of my life as if I don't matter." I ended somewhere around, "I want a relationship with you. I'm going to make an effort, but I need you to do the same." With those words and everything in between, I'd finally gotten it all off my chest. He listened and made some acknowledgments about his wrongdoings. We embraced, finished dinner, and our relationship began to change over time.

When he was in the States, he'd call and check on me. He also continued to send me Valentine's Day cards. We spent our first Thanksgiving weekend together in year three of my healing journey. By then, he'd moved to Atlanta, Georgia. Our plan for the weekend was to cook an African feast; I wanted to learn how to make dishes I'd enjoyed whenever we connected. Besides, he's a great cook, and like him, I love to cook. I have flashes of memories of my father cooking with a kitchen towel thrown over his shoulder when I was a kid. I remember sitting on the floor watching cartoons and him putting a huge plate of food in front of me. I'd demolish a plate of African stew and white rice like an adult. So, when we made plans to cook together that year, it was significant to me and took me back to rare memories from my childhood.

He drove over eight hours to see and spend time with me. I'd never seen that much effort from him. His commitment to see this through gave me hope. When he arrived, he took the guest bedroom in my house and chatted a bit before going to sleep. We rose early to go grocery shopping. We made Sierra Leonean-style jollof rice, pepper chicken, beef stew, potato leaves, and white rice. He was the executive chef and called me his sous chef; I soaked up as much of his cooking style and seasoning secrets as I could. We laughed and joked the whole day. It was a day that I yearned for as a girl, a day I didn't get until I was 33. We took the food to my mom's house to enjoy with family. When we arrived, my family was front and center, ready to greet my father after many years but also eager to enjoy an African-style dinner. I enjoyed spending time with him amongst family and friends. It was an evening filled with lots of food, fun, and laughs. That weekend with my father was one of my most enjoyable father-daughter memories I have to cherish. It was his effort, sincerity, and our time together that offered me the greatest sense of solace. Though I spent a short time with my father, that time gave my heart rhythm a jolt of steadiness I needed to continue to heal. Since then, we've had some challenges, but we've also had some great moments of coming together to include verbal expressions of love.

It wasn't until I accepted him and what he could offer that I shifted my mindset from idealism to reality. Truth is . . . he couldn't be the father I desired. He could only offer what was modeled to him because he lost his father when he was just a young man. Despite the time it took to forgive my father and heal from my childhood pain, one hard but open and honest conversation thrust me closer to true forgiveness over time. I can't say that it was easy. I can't say that it was quick. I can't say that we didn't argue—two strong-headed Africans, who are more alike than we even know. I can, however, say that I forgave him and found a level of respect for him as my father. I can say that I call him Dad even though I shuddered at the thought of the word leaving my mouth in previous years. I can say that I genuinely enjoy spending time with him and checking on him to see how he's doing. I can say that we've spent more time together since that conversation. I can say that I looked forward to his annual Valentine's Day cards during my singleness. I can say that he walked me down the aisle with my mother on the day of my wedding, although I cringed at the thought in years past. I can say that time has healed the wound, and we grow closer with each year. I can say that I'm the product of an absent father, but I'm also the product of father-daughter reconciliation, healing, and forgiveness.

Glimpses of Light

I was, however, not alone in my healing journey. There were always glimpses of light in dark spaces. Looking back on this time in my life, there was so much light guiding my path, and for that, I am grateful. I must acknowledge the emotional and spiritual midwives and bonus dads who helped me along the way. At every stage in my transformative process, I recognize those who were strategically placed in my path to help me—see life from a whole new perspective, enhance my prayer life, study scriptures relevant to my situation, finish my doctoral program, and serve as surrogate fathers. Midwives, experienced, faith-filled women, were sent directly to me to help me shift, transcend, and, as Iyanla Vanzant says, "interrupt the pattern" in my life.

Much like that transformative hug I received on that Saturday morning at church, midwives like her offered me emotional relief and wise counsel in all aspects of my life. I acknowledge them for helping me through my transformative process—from broken to mended, from hurt to healed, from sad to happy, from negative mindset to positive outlook, from then to now. I honor them for seeing me and helping me reach back into my past to help me heal forward.

Then, there were bonus dads all around me—surrogates. They'd show up in my life and give me physical relief through presence. My stepfather wasn't perfect. Even though he and my mother's relationship didn't work out, he was consistent in my life beginning at about five years old— taught me how to ride a bike, offered the wisdom he had, never missed a birthday or special occasion. My childhood was shaped in so many ways by his influence in ways that didn't speak to my fatherless void. The pain of my father's absence was so great that I couldn't find the courage to call him Dad in his presence. I was more comfortable with his nickname, Big Tony, and that seemed to be enough for him. Our relationship didn't reach the closeness that he and my sisters had . . . they were daddy's girls until his passing. Yet, his active presence and participation in my life offered me the stability of a male figure. I knew I could count on him not to be another one who left.

Whatever my stepfather couldn't give me, my church dad stepped in and gave me another perspective of fatherhood. I have no idea when I started calling him my church dad, but I think it started when I was trying to distinguish between him and other male figures in my life. We went to the same church for many years, and thus the name was born. *He has no idea I call him my church dad.* I was close to his wife, who was also a midwife for me. She was one of the ones who helped develop some of my early leadership and public speaking skills during my college years. When she died, I'd check on my church dad often. He was one of my go-to's for advice about men, a ball of wisdom. I often found myself stopping by his office after work. We'd talk for hours about God, life, love, relationships, and travel. He literally brokered deals for me to finance two of my cars. I felt a great sense of comfort around him—the safety of a father.

When I purchased my first home, I soon found out that I had squirrels living in my attic! Imagine being home alone and waking up to the sound of what you think are steel trash cans colliding outside on a windy day, only to find out that squirrels have eaten through your roof and fallen between the walls in your bathroom. Talk about a scary feeling. Once I realized that an animal had eaten its way into the house, I immediately contacted a pest control company. I was met hours later by the owner of the company, who saw how scared and afraid I was. He said, "You know what . . . you remind me of my daughter. I'm going to treat you like my daughter. It's going to be okay." I could've shed a thousand tears at that moment. He knew me from nowhere, saw me and wanted to help me for little to no money. He worked with me for months to trap squirrels that had six babies in the inaccessible part of my attic.

To most, this moment is just another woe in the life of a homeowner. Although I've had other moments where I've been helped when in need, this interaction with a pest control man honestly healed me in some way. Too often, I felt alone. My mother and grandmother were there, but I still felt alone, especially when it came to things that I felt like a man should do or be a part of. In those instances, I had to figure things out on my own. This incident with the squirrels in my attic was no different. But, when he uttered those words, "I'm going to treat you like you're my daughter," it was as if God was speaking to me. *I've got you. Don't you see I've always been there for you . . . helping and guiding you. It's going to be okay. Your father's not here, but I am.* In that moment, this man's words allowed me to see, for the first time, the goodness around me that I'd been overlooking for so long. Despite the father who left, God was sending what I needed when I needed it. Although it didn't seem like it at the time, I began to realize and embrace God as my father and through the presence of bonus dads, I came to acknowledge how I needed to be fathered. I needed a sense of safety, security, commitment, and guidance that didn't come packaged the way I might have wanted, but it came, nonetheless, in its own way. Whether it was in the form of a midwife or a bonus dad, I was being helped along my journey, although I hadn't realized all the light surrounding, guiding, and helping me along my path.

Heart Checkup

As I grew stronger in my faith and emotionally, I began to recognize that I was unwittingly practicing introspection, mostly when I was driving on the expressway with few cars on the road. There's just something about a near-empty expressway, driving at 70 miles per hour, with no music that takes me into fruitful thought. I low-key relish moments of self-reflection that cause me to question where I am, how I've grown, and lead me to new thoughts about myself. Heart checkups forced me to tell myself the truth, even when negative perceptions attempted to interrupt my thoughts. *How are you really feeling? God, I still hurt. My heart's still broken . . . still weak. I'm sad, not about him, but because the idea of him is not there. I still have insecurities. How did I contribute to this situation? I hinged my life on a timeline that didn't align with God's timing. That was your first mistake. Your second mistake was not hearing God for yourself about whether you were even supposed to be with this man.* With that, I'd turn up my car stereo system volume, switch to Bluetooth and search for a playlist. At times, the truth hurts, and I've often needed to pace myself when identifying it. It was in these moments that I acknowledged the irregularity of my heart rate, gained clarity, and strategized about approaches to emotional wellness. It was also in these moments that I recognized that I needed to continue shifting my mindset, rather than dwelling on the pain of heartbreak and feelings of dread that caused me to fear my future, in particular a future without a mate. The difference here was I was continuously turning to my daily devotional time for peace and comfort, journaling, acknowledging error, forgiving, and challenging negative perceptions.

Decisions, Decisions, Decisions

Settling into singleness comes with serious choices, especially when there's a strong desire for marriage. For me, I desired to marry, but I wasn't emotionally ready to start dating until perhaps year four of my healing journey. My heart checkups told me so. Instead of focusing on dating and marriage, I thrust myself into everything I hoped would help shape my future self—good distractions. While I healed emotionally, I turned toward my career, education, and living life without regret and distraction. Community service allowed me to give back and share some of my life lessons learned, but it also fed my spirit in so many ways. Although success in all those areas was around me, managing my emotions was no easy feat. I had to make a firm decision and commitment, when I decided to overcome my desire for marriage and redirect my attention. I became my own advocate and came up with a strategy. *Things just make more sense to me when I have a plan in place.* Without a strategy, I knew how easy it could be to fall into traps and succumb to misinformation. I began by asking myself,

- Who are you?

- What is your purpose?

- What were you born to do and become?

- Will you achieve your purpose, even if that purpose doesn't include marriage?

When I was able to focus on myself for the purpose of answering these questions honestly, I began to shift my mind from a focus on my life with a husband to a focus on life, even if it didn't include a husband. As I continued to enhance my relationship with God through prayer, devotional time, and document answers to my questions in my journal, the pace of my heart rhythm began to slow down to a more reasonable beat over time. Anxiety and fear started slowly diminishing. From there, I was able to make some decisions that helped me advocate for my time and my peace. The power of my recovery and my evolution was launched with focus, intent on reshaping my whole person—body, mind, spirit, and soul.

Prayer, meditation, fasting, and service to others were taking care of my mind, spirit, and soul work. My upbringing gave me the foundation to help my body recover, and I knew the benefits of clean eating and exercise. I grew up pescatarian and actively took dance classes, rode bikes, and did laps in my roller skates around my mom's basement. My siblings and I spent many weekends at my mom's aerobics classes and at farmers' markets all over Maryland, or swimming and riding bikes with my stepfather, who never really drove a car. He rode his bike everywhere; in another life, he probably could've been a professional cyclist. It was nothing for my mom to have mason jars full of fresh apple, pear, and orange juice in our freezer. Although we ate some seafood, we weren't like those people who say they are vegetarian just because they don't eat meat. My mom had us eating tofu hot dogs and sweet potato pie made with honey or turbinado. We ate whole grain bread that I could swear had seeds in it. We didn't eat peanut butter and jelly; we ate freshly ground chunky peanut butter with honey. *I think you get the point.* I retained some of my childhood eating habits into my adulthood, but I became a bit lax with eating lots of sugary foods and some poultry.

As part of my healing process, I turned back to my nutritional roots. I knew how powerful and healing a healthy diet filled with fresh fruits and vegetables could be to the body. So, I started juicing. I researched foods that supported emotional health in the areas of inner peace, eliminating depression, and ridding the body of toxins. In my quest, I learned more about vitamins, and the healing properties of various foods that not only supported emotional wellness but also improved the overall health of my body. I also drank nearly a gallon of water a day. I juiced fruits in the morning and drank vegetable juice at night.

I was detoxing emotionally and physically. I also joined a gym. At least four times a week for no less than 90 minutes, I hit the gym ready for pilates, spin class, Zumba, kickboxing, or strength training. Visiting the gym became one of my favorite pastimes. Movement that didn't feel like exercise was also one of my go-to's. I spent my free time at drop-in community dance workshops once a week or volunteering at youth organizations within my local community. Dance always made me feel I was ascending and that feeling gave me a sense of freedom from the world around me.

Table for One

I couldn't truly answer my self-directed questions about who I was and my purpose, despite the promise of a mate, without dating and loving me first. Redirecting my focus meant focusing on my relationship with God and embracing good distractions that led me to discover myself aside and apart from other people. Who was I when I was alone? Who was I without my best girlfriend by my side? Who was I amongst a crowd of people I didn't know? I didn't know entirely. I started dating myself. From the time I started liking boys in high school, there was some guy I was talking to on the phone or dating. Who was I without the phone calls and text messages that I often used to pass the time, until I met someone who really piqued my interest? I didn't know.

At times, I can be a bit of a loner. I was 15 the first time I took myself out to eat. I worked at McDonald's in high school. Instead of having my usual filet-o-fish sandwich with no tartar sauce, that day, I decided to walk across the street and have lunch at Friendly's. It was a family-friendly restaurant known for burgers and homemade ice cream. Just as soon as I walked in the door with my McDonald's uniform on, the hostess asked me if I wanted to dine-in or have carryout. I chose a table for one and ordered a grilled cheese sandwich and strawberry ice cream. I remember feeling so accomplished. It was the first time I ate at a restaurant alone and paid my own bill.

The next time I was bold enough to date myself, I was 29. When I looked around in my late twenties and early thirties, my friends were married, in committed relationships, had children, or simply had other plans when I wanted to hang out. I had to make a decision. Did I want to call the guy that I wasn't really interested in to hang out? Or, should I go at it alone and see what happened? I opted for the latter a lot.

Once, my job hosted an all-white dinner cruise on the Spirit of Baltimore at the downtown Inner Harbor. All my girlfriends were busy. I still wanted to go. So, I went by myself and had a great time. I even met a guy that night. We just talked, danced, and had a good time with my co-workers. We didn't even exchange numbers. The joy of that night was not in meeting him. I found joy in my decision to go to the white party alone without fear. It represented one of the moments when I chose to live life no matter what, or who was with me. That experience also taught me that unless I planned to date online or cozy up to the cable guy, mail man, or delivery man, I needed to embrace a free-spirited life, despite friends or romance. To add, with all my friends married and most with children, I needed to live my life. I couldn't be governed by their availability when I wanted to do something. It also taught me not to live in fear of being alone. Just because I go somewhere alone doesn't mean I'm lonely. There is a difference. If I was going to truly conquer my fear, I needed to strengthen my emotional intelligence, which meant embodying the capacity to be aware of and control my feelings. Taking control of my emotions meant facing my fear of being alone—fear of doing things alone, fear of not getting married, and fear, fear, fear . . . period.

For too long, fear guided decisions that caused me to jump into relationships too soon and settle for relationships that were less than God's best for me. Fear had me lost in my emotions and a desire for marriage. I could no longer be controlled by fear. And, if the man of my dreams never came or took a little longer than I expected, what next? Should I have sold my ticket to the white party and stayed home? No. Should I have postponed my trip to Paris? No, I did that in year three of my journey. Should I have ordered carryout instead of dining in alone? No, I often chose dinner and a movie for one, not because my girlfriends weren't available, but because I was dating and learning myself. Should I have believed the lies about singleness? Of course not. My singleness journey was mine to own and explore, despite the perpetual lies I once told myself, how trauma spoke to me, and societal ideals I was combatting.

Now, I understand the importance of the scriptures found in the Song of Solomon that admonish us several times "not to awaken love until the time is right" (2:7). The Song of Solomon is filled with wisdom about marriage and love, not only from God but also from a spouse. In it, I find that the charge not to awaken love too soon or before being able to handle all that comes along with love and relationships speaks to my plight as a single woman. This scripture turns a mirror on my life in ways that personify love awakened too soon and before I could handle it. I wasn't allowing a healthy, God-given love to awaken on its own, and for my haste, I suffered through great heartache and heartbreak.

This level of transformational thought and devotion to my process caused me to reconsider my thoughts about life, love, and the pursuit of happiness. The true beauty of the scream that I released all those years ago was the peace and steadiness I found in my heart, mind, soul, and spirit. That day, I made my pain audible. I'd buried it so deep that it had no choice but to come out as a scream.

Similarly, I have a greater connection to Ruth and Boaz's biblical story. Ruth showed me how to redirect my attention in the midst of life-altering circumstances toward finding emotional stability in love. For me, it wasn't until I dedicated my life to understanding and learning to love all of me that I was able to begin again with a new and fresh perspective about life and all it had to offer me. The time I spent falling in love with me opened the door to forgiveness, reconciliation, and a new sense of self helped me shift the trajectory of my life. Although I had many tough moments, the peace I was granted when I began to focus on myself without interruption was the greatest gift. And to think, all this awakening, revelation, and transformation are echoes from a scream still wisping in the wind, helping me keep the pace of my steady heart rhythm.

A Letter to Heartbreak: A Journal Entry Turned Social Media Post

Dear Heartbreak:

Sometimes, I felt like you threw a dagger into my heart. You made me feel like I wouldn't survive singleness. You didn't physically touch or beat me, but sometimes I felt like you did. I've experienced you in different forms. But, relationship heartbreak was much different because of the time, energy, and emotions I put into men who I never should've granted access to my heart.

Because of you, I've learned that I needed you because you helped strengthen my relationship with Christ, shape my character, and save me from a path that was never meant for me. In those moments of distress and overflows of powerful emotion, you, Heartbreak, certainly didn't feel like you were necessary. But, I'll take an experience with you over aborting my destiny for a man who had no place or served no true purpose in my life any day.

Heartbreak, you aren't easy to deal with at all. But, I learned that I needed to work through my healing journey in a God-focused, healthy manner to mend my heart. In doing so, you helped to thrust me into healing and wholeness. So, I thank God for you, Heartbreak. God used you to help me.

Most Sincerely,
Jasmine

Part 3

HAPPILY EVER AFTER

SIX

Mirror, Mirror on the Wall

It was 2013 when BET's *Being Mary Jane*, a TV drama series, aired. It detailed the complexities of the driven, professional black female experience, as seen through the life of Mary Jane Paul (Gabrielle Union), a television news anchor. Mary Jane is portrayed as strong and fearless, and yet she also has a vulnerable side. Although she was at the top of her game professionally, she wrestled with singleness in ways that left her jumping from one relationship to the next causing her to make some questionable decisions, as she toggled between men who were married, single, or mere crushes. In my opinion, she does so before settling the circumstances of her past in ways that leave her fully equipped to embrace, recognize, and attract a lasting love and relationship in her life sooner than the show's conclusion.

Like many other women, I tuned in each week to see how Mary Jane navigated through her family, career, and relationship experiences. Whether the episodes had me on the edge of my seat, clutching my pearls, or expressing tearful emotions, I loved the way Mary Jane came across the screen. She had a chic and sassy style, while she also brought some sense of normalcy to my own experiences as a single black female who has everything going for her. Though the complicated status as single toiled physically and emotionally against itself and the world around her, Mary Jane was resilient.

Year two of my healing journey began in 2013. I was 32, single, and embarking upon one of the highlights of my career. I'd just started working for two of President Barack Obama's political appointees, as a speechwriter for the Social Security Administration's acting commissioner and senior policy advisor to the commissioner's principal senior advisor. Although my frequent 90-minute commutes to and from D.C., speechwriting, and action items toward fulfilling the mandates of White House executive orders filled my 10-hour workdays, it was my morning prep work that kept me focused on my personal healing journey toward wholeness and a new sense of self. Though I'd reached a highlight in my career, I wouldn't have survived without the soul maintenance of mirror talk and devotional time with God at 5:00 a.m.

If I wasn't already staring at my bedroom ceiling at 4:30 a.m., with my tearful eyes, thinking about my present or past moments, like clockwork, my cell phone alarm started sounding at 4:45 a.m. I'd hit the snooze button on my touch screen, borrowing ten more minutes of sleep. It rang again at 5:00 a.m., and I was up and ready to devote my time to my self-care for at least an hour before it was time to get started with my day. Mornings began in my *Daily Walk Bible*, a devotional Bible designed to guide readers through the Bible in one year. In prayer, I laid my petitions before God and offered prayers of thanksgiving and praise. *Lord, thank you for healing me from the inside out. Thank you for healing my broken heart and binding all my wounds. I praise you for a future where I am genuinely happy, healed, and whole. I praise you, Lord, for saving me from myself.*

Year one and two of my journey focused on drying the tears of my past breakups, failures, disappointments, and shortcomings, while also steadying my emotions. I took the time to understand myself and why I made some of my worst decisions. It was also about being brutally open and honest with myself about my misguided focus and greatest challenges. I read the Bible and lots of self-help books. I found myself in year two better but not well. I was, however, less distracted with marriage, having completed graduate school and totally consumed with work—a good distraction.

By the end of year one, I, like Mary Jane, had decorated my mirrors and walls with Post-it Notes, as if they were journal entries. I jotted down encouraging scriptures and affirmations that covered my bedroom mirror like wallpaper, with just enough space to apply my MAC Studio Fix C7 foundation every morning. When the bedroom mirror filled, I plastered affirmation Post-its on nearly every door that I entered and exited. Feverishly, I'd grab my Post-its and write encouraging scriptures down that caught my attention during my devotional time. Those Post-its became a diversion from the moments where I felt at my lowest. I'd also write down anything that challenged negative thinking and tried to creep into my thoughts to make me relive my past. I'm an auditory learner. Almost without thinking, I started reading my Post-its aloud. Whether I was taking laundry down into the basement or walking out the door for work, I couldn't escape them where I'd strategically placed them. Affirmations helped me speak positively to myself until I heard, believed, or it manifested. By manifesting I mean I spoke until I saw a significant change in my thoughts and opinions about my life and future. As I spoke over myself, my heart rhythm and emotions began to shift. My conversations changed. My thoughts changed. Anxiety turned to peace. Tears turned to a genuine smile and outward displays of joy. Mirror talk was my emotional maintenance; it helped denounce everything that held me captive in my mind, heart, and spirit.

Affirmations for Brokenness

Don't let your hearts be troubled. Trust in
God, and trust also in me. (John 14:1)

- I'm no longer broken but healed and whole.

- God is mending my broken heart.

- I face challenges with strength and wisdom.

- I will live my life without dwelling on and in my past.

Affirmations for Healing

*The Lord is close to the brokenhearted; he
rescues those whose spirits are crushed.*
(Psalms 34:18)

- I am healed.

- I give myself permission to forgive everything.

- I'm healing with each step forward I take.

- I have confidence in God to be completely healed.

- I'm not bitter but becoming better.

- Let it go.

Affirmations for Love

*Love is patient and kind. Love is not jealous or boastful
or proud or rude. It does not demand its own way. It is
not irritable, and it keeps no record of being wronged. It
does not rejoice about injustice but rejoices whenever the
truth wins out. Love never gives up, never loses faith, is
always hopeful, and endures through every circumstance.*
(1 Corinthians 13:4-7)

- I love me a whole lot.

- I'm loved by God.

- God is my father, and He loves me so much.

- I've never been rejected by God.

- My family loves and supports me.

- I'm not perfect, but God loves me still and always.

Affirmations for Happiness

> *Take delight in the Lord, and he will give
> you your heart's desires.* (Psalm 37:4)

- I'm happy no matter the circumstance.

- I control and own my happiness.

- My happiness is not dependent on a man.

- I'm whole, healed, happy, and prospering emotionally, physically, and spiritually.

Affirmations for the Future

> *"For I know the plans I have for you," says the Lord.
> "They are plans for good and not for disaster, to give
> you a future and a hope. . ."* (Jeremiah 29:11)

- I'm not afraid of my future.

- I'm closer to my God-intended destiny and purpose with every breath and step.

- I don't settle for less than God's best for me.

- I will meet my God-intended mate in God's timing.

- My future's so bright.

- I'm excited about my future.

By the time *Being Mary Jane's* season finale aired in 2019, viewers had seen Mary Jane's evolution. We saw her through triumphs and struggles, romance, office politics, and familial drama, while also watching her follow through with some difficult choices that all lead to her eventual marriage. While this television adaptation is total fiction, it was the manner in which art imitated life that had women tuned in from week to week, in addition to the drama-filled storyline. I'm sure that there were many women whose lives resonated with Mary Jane's life. I recognize through her storyline the significance of how the choices we make can define our future positively or negatively. I also acknowledge the essence of how influential mirror talk was to my emotional maintenance and steadiness.

Though a bit regimented, because that's how my mind works, my process was my process. Through it, I thanked God that I didn't let anger and bitterness hold me hostage to the point of festering negative thoughts that could overtake my mind. I'm also thankful for having the courage to do the work required to overcome the feelings of abandonment and rejection that caused me to attract the wrong type of man. It was mirror talk that helped me steady my heart rhythm, while also helping me to avoid living with insecurities about beauty, weight gain, or anything else. With the help of God, I combatted negative self-talk with positivity.

I am a gift from God.
I am loved.
I am pretty enough.
I am just the right size.
I can have a relationship with my father
without reliving the past.
I can never be abandoned because God is always with me.
I am because God says I am.
I am my husband's favor.
I am enough.

And, though experiential triggers can catch anybody off guard and surface in the most inopportune times, I recognized my growth every time I was able to pinpoint my triggers quickly. It was in year four of my healing and growth journey that I started recognizing my triggers. In 2014, I became what I thought was deathly ill. I'd started to have severe gallbladder attacks and fibroids that were detected in my early twenties. Two centimeters grew into large masses that caused me great pain, even when I wasn't menstruating. Long story short, my hormones were going crazy, and there was a connection between the gallbladder attacks and the rapid growth of the fibroids. To help support what doctors advised, I started seeing a naturopathic doctor who practiced in the United States and Africa.

With his help, my health started improving after about a year of working with him. In need of a follow-up appointment, I called him during a break at work and left a message when there was no answer. I followed up with a text message when I didn't get a call back in 24 hours. After several busy days, about a week later, I remembered that I hadn't heard from him about my appointment. In that moment, this overwhelming sense of sadness came upon me. My thoughts shifted to everything but, *Maybe he's out of the country.* Instead, I thought, *He doesn't want to be my doctor anymore. He doesn't want to help me. What am I going to do now?* Just as soon as my thoughts began to swirl in my head, I recognized one of my strongest triggers—feeling left or cast aside by men, a type of social rejection. Even though I'd forgiven my father and we were in a much better place. I was triggered because my naturopathic doctor hadn't contacted me as soon as I would've liked. Even though I knew he often traveled to remote parts of Africa, not once did this dawn on me. And to think, no more than one day later, after I'd identified my trigger point, my doctor called me to apologize for not contacting me sooner. He explained that he was in Africa and, in his words, had "spotty reception," leaving him unable to make any phone calls.

It's amazing just how quickly negative thinking can cause an emotional spiral down the wrong path. Although this moment in time with my doctor would've thrown me off-kilter, I like to think that my intentional focus on reshaping my mindset mentally, emotionally, and spiritually allowed me to pinpoint this trigger. Active demonstration of positive reinforcement took years to master, but I was determined not to live in a place of negativity. There are moments, even now, years later, that trigger me, but I've learned to shift gears quickly. Sincere, focused efforts that began with acknowledging my complications, dedicating devotional time to God, recognizing glimpses of light around me, and sustaining myself by becoming my own advocate ended with managing my soul maintenance through mirror talk.

SEVEN

Ivory Blusher

♥

Nothing I dreamt of or longed for when I started planning my wedding happened. Everything was different than I imagined. A quick screenshot from Pinterest inspired my wedding colors. I had a real-life "Say Yes to the Dress" moment in the bridal salon when I selected my wedding dress, which came with a side of tears. Who knew I'd cry real tears when I found my dress? Who knew the "planzilla" would decide to purchase her dress the same day after just trying on ten dresses? I didn't. I thought I'd at least explore three more bridal stores and try on near a hundred dresses before I made a decision. Both actions were out of character. The three-tier wedding cake with a faux bottom tier was a hit with the wedding guests. They never knew the hotel caterer was cutting the real wedding cake somewhere in their kitchen. I'm convinced now that an $800 cake tastes just as good as a $3,000 wedding cake. Sis, order the faux cake, save your coins, and keep it moving. The ivory chapel length veil with blusher totaled $27.00, including tax and shipping from China. My veil was just as beautiful as those $500 veils in the bridal store that I was never going to purchase.

Bottom line: What I thought I wanted when I had those, "When I get married" discussions with my girlfriends years ago was different when I faced the reality of planning a wedding. By this time, I was a different person. I'd imagined glitz and glam and sparing no expense when trying to achieve the "look" I wanted, perhaps something you'd find in a magazine or at a celebrity wedding. Even though we achieved the "look," and married at the Marriott Marquis, the largest black-owned hotel in D.C., we made no sudden moves when invoices for decor came in at over $8,000. We then decided to make decisions based on planning for our future not a wedding. With the fantasy of wedding planning in my rearview, what actually evolved far exceeded our expectations. An entire wedding weekend that started with a traditional African wedding ceremony and party on Friday night. Then, there was Saturday morning hair prep, afternoon wedding rehearsal, and the bachelorette party at The Park at 14th in N.W., D.C. We concluded with a noonday wedding ceremony and Sunday brunch. It was a weekend to remember. It was perfectly, perfect, just like the day we met and the days that followed.

Have you ever whispered a quick prayer in the middle of the day when everything and everyone is moving all around you? Perhaps you are right in the middle of your next work meeting or conversation with a coworker, and a thought crosses your mind that leads to one of those quick internal prayers. You know, like when a random thought comes to your mind, and you turn that thought into a prayer that lasts mere seconds. Well, I have. I don't do it often, but I'm convinced that those one-second, minimalist prayers work. They work just as much as those that begin with flowery words and follow the how-to's of prayer that I learned in Sunday school as a child.

It was 2015, and year four of my healing journey. I can't recall where I was or what I was doing, but I do remember whispering, "God, I'm ready to start dating again." It had been years since I'd actively dated. Life was hectic at times, so I shut down to work on myself, focus on busy workdays, deal with sudden sickness, and have a social life with family and friends. I checked the cadence of my heartbeat and realized I had a steady pulse and maintained my pace by sticking to what worked for me. I was good and feeling ready to start dating.

Dating had new meaning by the time I started again in 2016. A timeline for marriage didn't drive me. My life's purpose did, and meeting someone who fit into and supported my purpose was one of the keys. By 2016, my relationship with God was solid. I knew who I was and how I wanted to show up in the world. I also had a ritual for how I'd maintained my heart rhythm. Through my soul work, I'd been able to really answer some hard questions before accepting any invitations to dinner or a movie. *Who are you? What is your purpose? What were you born to do and become? Will you achieve your purpose, even if that purpose doesn't include marriage?*

In learning and defining myself, I aimed simply to use my best skills and talents to serve and support others. But, what exactly did that purpose statement translate to in my life? Once I examined my life aside from the struggles I had with singleness, I found that I was already actively engaged in activities that supported how I wanted to show up in the world. I'd dedicated many years to teaching as an adjunct faculty member where I felt I was most needed, historically black colleges and universities. I got my start at Coppin State University and later taught at my alma mater, Morgan State University. Whether I was volunteering within my community for youth organizations, exploring the countryside on mission trips to South Africa, or pursuing a career in public service, I aimed to show up in the world as a servant leader who used my best skills and talents to transform lives for the better. These are the activities that feed my soul in ways that money can't buy. It was with my life's purpose in full view that I felt prepared to accept someone else into my life who could support me. Likewise, I could support whatever he set out to do.

In Spring 2016, I was accepted into a six-month leadership development program, the President's Management Council Fellows Program in D.C. I completed my assignment at the U.S. Department of Energy. It was a 55-minute commute from Baltimore on an average day in the car. But, a two-hour commute during rush hour traffic, if my 4:00 a.m. wake-up call didn't have me racing through my house trying to ensure I'd catch the 6:25 a.m. express MARC train to D.C. It was a beautiful experience to work in the District in Spring 2016. I was just in time for lots of afternoon professional meetups and networking events, lunchtime walks along the National Mall, and great weather that made my commute easy.

The dating scene, however, had changed. By this time, online dating was even more of a thing, and social media was where I got my news and the deets regarding anything that was happening in the world. Texting was the primary mode of communication during the getting-to-know-you phase, and a WYD *(What You Doin')?* text message was considered a conversation starter. But, I was game and had proclaimed to my girlfriends that I'd try online dating by 36 if I hadn't met anyone worth my time. It was like clockwork when I began my detail that I started meeting new prospects. Whether on the MARC train or at networking events, I was now open to something new, and with the right intentions, my openness started getting responses. I'd shifted my desire for a mate from ingrained ideals driven by the Cinderella Complex to desiring a mate who could add value to my already-defined purpose, goals, dreams, and aspirations in life. I didn't aim to have a man fill a void or validate my beauty or womanhood but rather to gain a life partner for companionship and support. I was purpose-driven, and my narrative on how I looked at life and relationships changed. Though I desired a husband, even if that never came into fruition, I knew that my purpose and direction in life would remain the same.

When I started dating, I met some pretty interesting men, and a few led to the exchange of numbers and conversations, although at least one led to a complete phone block. Me and Mr. Block communicated via text for a little while before things got creepy; he kept asking me to send him pictures. For what? He got irritated with me when I didn't. Like why do you need my picture? I saw him almost every day in passing in D.C. Through casual conversations, I'd heard something about men wanting women to send them pictures. I didn't know if he wanted a naked picture or a selfie. I didn't get it, nor did I understand why he started getting upset on the phone. It was a no for me. Block.

My preference during this time was the tea or coffee meetup. If I was asked out, I'd recommend we meet for tea or coffee for my own selfish reasons. I felt it less intense and gave us a chance to get acquainted without the pressure of the traditional first date. And, if I didn't care for pursuing a romantic relationship just based on his conversation alone, I could leave the interaction at tea or coffee without having to sit through an entire dinner.

I did, however, accept one dinner date. He was Nigerian, handsome, kind, attentive, goal-oriented, and driven by his faith in God. He had great conversation, but I couldn't see myself with him. He was too young for me. I was nearly eight years older than him. He was at the beginning stage of everything in his life, just finishing college, starting a new job, and living with his mother. Nothing wrong with any of it, but we were in two different places in life. He also seemed a little passive. I have a strong personality, and I need my man to gather me up and take the lead when necessary so I don't overpower him. Plus, chilling out at his mother's house watching Netflix would not have felt right. I was ready to date someone with the intent to marry, and he wasn't there yet and needed time. Every human deserves the space and time to evolve. We kept in touch for a little while after what was a great dinner but nothing materialized because I didn't reach back to meet his advances.

> "Every human deserves the space and time to evolve."

Just before my development program ended in September 2016, I'd decided to attend the Congressional Black Caucus' annual conference. Every year, for five days in September, African-American politicians and thought leaders from every industry come together to discuss policy and put forward strategic plans for the advancements of black politics, social justice, economics, business, education, and health care, among other things. It's one of the leading conferences that seeks to use its platform to make a sincere impact on issues that concern African Americans nationally and internationally. The who's who of influence in black political power and economics take over D.C., to collaborate, offer insights, and lay out the path forward.

In years past, I hung out with friends at the evening receptions and parties. This time, I was determined to take some time away from work to attend the day sessions. My career and personal endeavors were leading me into different spheres, and I felt a compelling sense of urgency to attend, even if that meant going alone. I made contact with friends who I thought would be interested, but no one followed up with an expression of interest. I persisted and decided to go alone. I registered for the Caucus, purchased a ticket to the Emerging Leaders Luncheon, and booked a hotel in D.C. Just before the Caucus, I learned through a Facebook post that one of my closest childhood friends planned to attend, which prompted me to text her to let her know I was also going. We connected and made our way to D.C. for the start of what turned out to be a great weekend.

We began our day exploring the Walter E. Washington Convention Center and figuring out which sessions we wanted to attend. We anticipated the start of the Emerging Leaders Luncheon, which was designed for young professionals to receive mentorship from industry leaders on various topics over lunch. My friend chose media mentorship, and I selected women in leadership. Just before noon, we made our way to the luncheon and then found our designated mentorship tables. I had an engaging, lively discussion with my mentor and nine other ladies, some of whom I still correspond with today. We discussed tips, tools, and strategies for advancing in our careers over lunch. It was a truly dynamic conversation that left me with takeaways that I still use.

At the end of the session, I stood searching the crowd for my friend amongst the hundreds of attendees. I spotted her with the media mentor and a few other attendees, taking selfies and pictures. She stood not far from Brian, the man who would become my husband just over two years later. As I approached my friend, eager to figure out what we were doing next, I was immediately introduced to Brian. We didn't lock eyes like in some type of on-screen romance. We had some small talk, and in moments, we'd all decided to stay connected throughout the Caucus, because there was so much going on that it was hard to keep up with all the events happening at the Convention Center and throughout the District. We'd all exchanged numbers. From there, that weekend was like a whirlwind. My friend, Brian, and I hung out during the entire Caucus, attending day sessions and evening receptions together. We had a great time going from one event to the next, networking, and meeting new people.

So, you may be asking how Brian and I evolved from a professional connection at the Caucus to husband and wife. Simply put, it was time for both of us to meet, date, and marry. We were both ready. I can't let the details of our story slide without symbolically inserting the praise hands emoji for the quick prayer I prayed a few months before meeting him. This time, the prayer was sparked by one of my closest friends. I think I said early on that I love to cook, and it's so fitting that I'd have a friend who loves to as well. We were swapping recipes at my house one Friday night. She had her authentic Jamaican recipes, and I had my West African recipes. Just before we started cleaning up for the night, she said, "Girl! I have this prayer book in my car I want you to check out." She got the book, turned to the page she wanted me to read and told me to read the prayer for a future husband. Then, she said, "When you get to the good part, let me know." I read about three pages or so of the prayer and found the part she was talking about. I hollered,

"Here it is . . . let my husband relocate to locate me!" I think we laughed for a good 30 minutes after repeating that part of the prayer about 20 times. What I thought was a shared laugh among two friends wasn't. Let me remind you that those quick prayers that last mere seconds do work. Several months later, I met Brian in D.C. on business all the way from Florida.

But, here's how we got started:

The day before the Caucus ended on Sunday of that year, Brian and I made plans to hang out on Saturday night. By this time, his cousin had arrived in town. My friend couldn't make it, but I'd made plans to bring along one of my closest male friends. He was my ride; I had no plans to drive to D.C. from Baltimore and back after midnight. I knew I'd be hanging out late. Brian and I planned to meet at 9:00 p.m. in the lobby of the Renaissance Hotel on 9th Street in Northwest, D.C.—one of the hangout spots for Caucus attendees. Not long after my friend and I arrived, Brian and his cousin also arrived, and we made introductions. We huddled in the lobby, trying to figure out what party we were going to attend first.

Before long, we had a full group of six; two other friends of friends joined us just before we called an UberX to take us to a party hosted by Google at the Smithsonian National Museum of African American Art in Southwest, D.C. We knew the event was ticketed, but we went anyway. We arrived and piled out of the UberX with ladies in cocktail dresses and heels, and the gents in suits and ties. We marched up to the gate trying to get into the event, and it was a no-go. Tickets were sold out. I happened to see a new associate that I'd met in D.C. during my detail. We greeted each other fondly and shared an embrace. I talked about how I just tried to get into the event, and I inquired with her about tickets. She explained that her sister worked with Google and might be able to get us into the party. I was game and let my group of friends know that we had a good chance of getting into the event. Within minutes of the exchange, my D.C. connection was waving at me to follow her into the party, with five other people with me no less. People were everywhere, the deejay was lit, and we were having a ball exploring the museum that had been turned into a club for the evening. We ate, danced, and took pictures. The girls hit the dance floor and the guys, as usual, stood around watching the girls dance. Although he hovered around me . . . possibly blocking any other prospects, Brian and I didn't get a dance in together that night, but the story gets better.

Not long after we got into the party, my friend's girlfriend called and told him that she'd been in an accident just outside of D.C.; she was on her way to meet us at the event. My friend caught an Uber back to his car and by this time, it was 12:30 a.m. I told my friend not to worry about me; I just wanted him to make sure she was okay. I was having so much fun that I hadn't even thought about not having a ride home. I figured I could catch an Uber home, if needed. Within an hour or so, my friend called and told me that he could come back and get me, but that he was at least 45 minutes away. The party was nearing its end. I didn't want to be standing around, waiting for him. By this time, I'd found a bench to sit on because my feet were hurting. Brian sat next to me and we got some time to talk alone. I explained what was happening and that I planned to call an Uber to take me home.

"I'll take you home," he said immediately.

"But, I live in Baltimore."

"I'm staying in Baltimore."

"I thought you were from Florida," I said quizzically.

"I'm here in town for a couple of weeks on business."

"Oh! Well, if you take me, you need to know that my friend knows exactly what you look like. I don't want you turning into some kinda stalker."

He laughed. "I'm not like that. I have to take my cousin to meet the person who's going to take her to the airport, but I can take you home." I agreed and that was the moment, I did something that I probably would never have done. I let Brian take me home. I felt comfortable because I'd spent the last few days getting to know him, and he seemed like a really nice guy. I honestly thought I'd never see him again because he lived in Florida, and if I did, it wouldn't be until next year's Caucus. He didn't drop me off until near 4:00 a.m. The party ended at 2:00 a.m. and we—me, Brian, and his cousin—caught an Uber back to Brian's car, about ten minutes away from the museum. We dropped his cousin off at a friend's house in Upper Marlboro, Maryland and had to wait 20 minutes before someone answered the door for her. From there, we headed straight to Baltimore, a 50-minute ride from Upper Marlboro. I can't tell you what we talked about on the ride, but when I got home, I thanked him and went straight into the house and crashed on the bed. Sleep was calling my name after several long days and nights in D.C.

As tired as I was, I got up, got dressed, and headed out to church for the 10:45 a.m. service. *When I lived at home with my mom, she never let me sleep in from church on the rare occasions when I did stay out late. I got a few hours of sleep and was up and getting ready.* As usual, the singing was great, and I anticipated a great message from my pastor. Next thing I know, it's offering time; I look up and Brian is being led around the church by the ushers to give his offering. He passes my row before he reaches the offering bucket, stops momentarily, and turns toward me, as if to say *ta-daaaa . . . here I am.* I mouthed the words, "What are you doing here?" to him as he walked around the church to give his offering. Shocked! I couldn't believe he came to my church. During our time together at the Caucus, we had a brief exchange about churches to visit in the area. My friend and I shared a few church names, including our home churches' names. Imagine my surprise when he showed up at my church. I didn't even see him write the name of the church down. I literally thought we were having small talk. When the service ended, I had the opportunity to introduce him to my mom and sisters. Since we're accustomed to having family dinner together, as a kind gesture, I asked Brian if he wanted to have dinner with us. Had I known that we'd start dating, I wouldn't have asked, until I knew it was serious. I never introduced men to my family, unless it was something serious and committed. I liked to vet them before they met the family. This time was different. I was being nice, since he said he was from out of town. But of course, he accepted the invitation. He'll never admit it, but he was definitely interested in me and wanted to spend as much time with me as possible while he was in town. This Sunday dinner was different than any other one. My aunt was in town visiting from Philadelphia, Pennsylvania for the weekend. We had a full table for dinner, my mom, two sisters, aunt, one of my aunt's sons, me, and Brian. I was sitting at dinner at Texas Roadhouse, a steakhouse restaurant chain, wondering how this man got a chance to meet my family just days after we'd met.

From that day on, we talked every day, all day; we texted during the day and talked for hours in the evening. We had our first date at a local seafood restaurant just a week later. We totally skipped the tea and coffee step that I'd set up for myself, but that didn't stop me from taking a few phone calls from two other men whom I'd given my number to at the Caucus. At this point, we were getting to know each other and that knowing could've led to a friendship or romance. We hadn't reached the decision-making stage as yet. I found him engaging, and I simply enjoyed talking to him and learning more about him. He challenged my thinking on multiple levels, from his ambition to his spirituality and business. Most of all, he wasn't intimidated by me, but rather he celebrated who I was and who I was becoming.

He had my attention when I asked and he answered my request for him to find a way to get us tickets to the newly built National Museum of African American History & Culture. So here's the catch, the museum had millions of people vying for tickets and trying to gain entry. Just the week before, President Obama led the museum opening ceremony and ticket access for the weeks and months that followed were nonexistent, according to the museum's website. But, this man, whom I'd met just two weeks prior, called me on that Saturday evening, asked me what I was doing, and told me he had the tickets to the museum. I couldn't believe it. All I could say was, "How did you get the tickets?" And, he said, "I'll tell you when I pick you up. I'm on the way back from D.C." My next move was to get dressed and ask questions later. He arrived just before 7:00 p.m., and we were off to the museum within the second week of its opening. I learned on the near one-hour ride, that he'd driven to D.C. that morning for a couple of meetings. While there, he stopped by the museum to see if there was any way he could get tickets. Well, apparently the museum set aside same-day tickets for those who physically came to the museum to request them. With our tickets in hand, hours before I knew he'd accomplished the mission I challenged him with, he'd committed to doing whatever it took to win my heart before I trusted him with it. He'd committed to seeing where things went with us before he really even knew me well enough to make a decision about trusting me with his heart.

So, let's recap. Brian drove to D.C. from Baltimore for a meeting, and stopped by the museum to see if there was any way he could get us tickets. He went to several meetings that day, drove back to Baltimore to pick me up, and drove back to D.C. Together, we explored the wonder within the museum, slowly taking it in with awe and expectation, each room we entered. From 8:00 p.m. until after midnight—*during the time when the museum offered extended hours*—we took in the newness with refreshing anticipation. It was amazing to see all the African-American history and cultural artifacts in one place, in celebration and honor of such a rich history. It truly was a wondrous experience that I was able to share with him—a special moment that still makes me smile.

I had this moment and others like it to cherish during our dating season. From this date, I was committed to seeing where this thing would go. For a short period after, I did have a few conversations with the two other men that I met at the Caucus. Nothing materialized with those other guys. Eventually I stopped following up with phone calls and texts, and so did they. Brian had my full attention. Though cautious, I was curious and wanted to see where things would go.

> *Above all else, guard your heart, for everything*
> *you do flows from it.* (Proverbs 4:23)

We dated, but for me, it was with a twist. I couldn't approach this relationship the same way I did in the past. I allowed God to remain the focus of my heart rather than the idea of marriage because I'd found my rhythm in God before Brian found me. We started dating in what some would call a traditional courtship—learning and growing together without the pressure of sexual intimacy clouding our true perceptions and thoughts about one another. Though challenging at times, abstinence was our choice—a choice I am grateful we had the grace to endure. I fell in love with his relationship with Christ, ambition, intellect, purpose, personality, and his expressions of love for me before sexual intimacy further enhanced my love for him in marriage. A few things helped me sustain and monitor my heart rhythm:

1. **Prayer.** Consistent communication with God through prayer and meditation helped keep me centered and focused on my purpose, while I was dating him.

2. **Openness.** Letting my guard down with openness was key. I couldn't be guarded and at the same time open to something new and different in my life. So I could receive love, I remained open enough not to let past hurts hold my mind and heart hostage.

3. **Pace.** It was so important for me not to get too carried away with my emotions and excitement about what was potentially an evolving relationship. Pace setting required taking the moment in, listening, and going with the flow. It required clarity about the phase of the relationship we were living in, rather than making assumptions about his intentions for or with me.

4. **Heart Check.** Introspection about how I was honestly feeling while dating him helped me

acknowledge where I was in my mind. I questioned myself often. Was I observing signs that would be problematic later? How did he make me feel about myself? Did I have to dumb myself down or dim my light around him?

5. **Truth.** I came clean about my past when I felt like I could trust him with it. I told the truth about who I was, leaving no secrets to carry into a relationship.

6. **Clarity.** I was clear that he wasn't the last man who hurt me, and I wasn't willing to hold the new man responsible for that old relationship.

7. **Discovery.** After I discovered who I was, I was pleased to sit, watch, and observe who he was around business associates, family, and friends. I wanted to discover and understand him, soaking in his essence. I paid close attention to how he treated and spoke to me. I watched for anything glaring that could potentially make me feel uncomfortable later. I also observed who I was around him to ensure that I could be myself around him.

8. **Enjoy.** I enjoyed a healthy dating relationship that wasn't driven by sexual intimacy. I enjoyed being in a relationship without thinking about marriage, even though I didn't plan to be a lifetime girlfriend. I let time take its course.

We dated for over two years before we were engaged, and then we married eight months later. It was his choice to marry where we met . . . right across the street from the

Convention Center at the Marriott Marquis. After all those years of waiting and longing for marriage, the time spent waiting and dating for him felt like a dream. Sometimes I couldn't believe I'd met someone I was in a relationship with where my peace wasn't compromised. Being with Brian made me feel safe in a relationship.

Someone asked me, not long after I was married, how I knew I married "the One." A question I'd never been asked. I paused for a few seconds before I responded.

"I felt so much peace in my heart and spirit about the relationship. There was no uncertainty in my heart." She just listened and never responded.

I wonder now what she may have thought about my response. Peace was a feeling I'd never encountered in past relationships. Peace. Months after we got into a committed relationship, I finally acknowledged what I'd call a good gut feeling. I think I felt that peace when Brian and I first met. I remember scanning the room at the Caucus' luncheon looking for my friend. When I saw Brian, I literally felt my spirit leap. I can't explain it. I can't define it. Whether you'd define it as a gut feeling or something supernatural, it was a feeling so prevalent that I said to myself, *What was that?* It was a feeling I never felt before, and one that I will always remember. I paused for mere seconds and brushed off the feeling to proceed with my day, not knowing that my life would be forever changed.

Throughout our courtship, I had the most amazing sense of peace. Anxiety and fear about the relationship were nonexistent, but they were apparent in past relationships. In the past, I never felt settled and always had this tingle in my gut. I'd feel an uneasiness that accompanied anxiety and questions. *God, is he "the One?" Will he accept my dreams and goals? Is he going to leave me like . . . ? Should I keep dating him?* To add, I honestly never felt like I could be myself in other relationships. It was like I had to hide some of my aspirations, hopes, dreams, and aspects of my personality.

In other relationships, I never felt a peace that allowed me to be carefree enough to really enjoy the date or relationship. My mind, heart, and spirit would never allow me to settle into those relationships. I literally wrestled within myself in past relationships because I was trying to force relationships that were never meant to be.

It took me longer than Brian to know that he was "the One" for me. I was cautious and wanted to be sure I was making the right decision. When he eventually asked me to be in a committed relationship after four months of dating, he said among other things, "When you find what you're looking for you stop looking." He acknowledged his intentions for and with me early on, without hesitation. I was more comfortable getting into a relationship with him than I'd ever been. Looking back, it was how I handled our courtship that let me know my heart rhythm was steady. For the first time, I could be myself. I wasn't overwhelmed by thoughts about marriage. I was able to maintain a focused relationship with Christ, be open to new possibilities without fear, and keep a safe pace without thinking about my timeline. I stuck to my soul maintenance regimen with care and consistency. I self-reflected and told him my truth with openness and clarity, while enjoying a fresh new relationship, without the veil of my past hindering my future.

Most of all, I didn't discuss marriage until he did. Even then, I wasn't holding on to him so tight that if things didn't work, I'd fall apart.

I was new. It wasn't dating and marriage that let me know I wasn't the same. It was peace.

Epilogue

On Being Steady

Matters of the heart are never easy. My success story is in how I was able to manage my feelings, without continuing to succumb to emotions that could've cut me off the bright future that I now see for myself. Although it took me years to find my rhythm in singleness, I celebrate the fact that I eventually found it.

I know conversations about love and marriage are decades old. I've had many discussions with women who desire marriage and am asked now more than I can count how I knew my husband was "the One." As discussions about love and relationships continue, what I'll offer as a final note is that everything in life has a rhythm. It's so important that we are aware of that to determine our own frequency in every facet of life.

Yet, my life rhythm is different now. As I write these words with just one year of marriage under my belt, I'm finding my rhythm as a married woman. Brian and I spent the last two months of our first year of marriage in quarantine. The Coronavirus caused a worldwide pandemic. Millions around the world sheltered-in-place for upwards of four months to help stop the spread of the virus. Although we faced times we'd never seen, we drew closer in quarantine—attending virtual church, reading books, riding bikes, playing games, and talking about our future together. Our first anniversary was one we'll never forget. We turned our dining room into a five-star dining experience, with white linen, candles, lobster and shrimp dinner, and a little R&B soul. We topped dinner off with the best anniversary cake, a moist bananas foster cake with caramel filling, as we watched our wedding video for the first time together.

Quarantine also offered me time for introspection, especially since I used a lot of my time to finish the first draft of this manuscript. I found my heart rhythm steady in many areas of my life. But, I couldn't for the life of me figure out why I was so hard on myself all those years ago. I'd accomplished a lot of good, and despite all my challenges, I focused on my blemishes and didn't give myself enough credit. Perhaps it was my upbringing, I often felt I had to be perfect, and meet my mother's standards, which often felt high. A grade of "B" should've been an "A." The freshly-mopped kitchen floor always needed another scrub. Perhaps I created success criteria for myself to please my absent father. *If I do X, he'll surely see me and want to be in my life.* Perhaps it's both . . . perhaps it's neither . . .

Needless to say, I recognize this part of me that has a

tendency not to stop and celebrate the victories as much as I dwell on what I considered failures. I also know that perfection is too far to reach, and I learned not to allow fear of any kind to overtake me with worry. Looking forward to celebrating many more wedding anniversaries, I'm more aware of who I am, which I believe will serve me well in marriage. To add, according to other married women I talk to, my rhythm as a wife will evolve and change as I change, as my husband changes, and as our family expands. As I evolve, I have as my foundation: confidence in God to see me through every circumstance, practical knowledge and strategies that work, and courage to face any challenge head-on without fear.

Looking toward this next phase of my life, I know that heart rhythms is a topic in which both single and married women can see themselves. I look forward to continuing this dialogue with other women. While I'll continue to support single women, I also look forward to understanding and embracing the evolving heart rhythms I'll feel during my marriage. It's my sincere hope that I've shared many conversation starters and writing prompts for women that will lead to the steadiness of not only their heart but also their minds, bodies, and souls. Whether you embrace journaling, self-help books, empowerment workshops, or therapy to support maintaining your wellness, I hope this book will serve as another trusted resource.

For single women still managing their heart rhythms, I offer my journal, *Heart Rhythms: A Guided Journal for Thriving in Singleness*, to help others facilitate their singleness with intentional introspection. This journal is designed to help single women explore and navigate the range of emotions and experiences while single and satisfied, single and waiting, or single and dating. Included are writing prompts, exercises, and free space for those who enjoy the freedom to express themselves artistically or in writing.

Lastly, in sharing my story about surviving singleness with you, I hope this book will and has helped you see your journey as a single woman differently. If you've found this book helpful and insightful, please share it with your best girlfriend, friend or family member, and recommend it to a book club or women's empowerment group. I'd be happy to learn more about how you connected with my story. Feel free to contact me at www.jasmineleighmorse.com and leave a book review on Amazon or Barnes & Noble.

Acknowledgments

When I sat down to write this book, I had no idea what would evolve. It was an act of faith that pushed me to spend countless hours writing about topics I never shared with anyone. I'm certain that I couldn't have completed this work without faith in my Lord and Savior, Jesus Christ. Lord, thank you for those 3:00 a.m. nudgings to wake up and write. Thank you for creative ideas and those soft whispers that let me know what to write next. I'm convinced now more than ever that every good and perfect gift comes from you (James 1:17).

I'm so blessed to have the love and support of my family. I'm especially grateful and thankful for my husband, Brian J. Morse. His love and unwavering support during the writing process was invaluable. Thank you for the space and time to write without interruption and for your motivation and thought-provoking feedback. My mother, Guana E. Williams, Esq., is one of my greatest champions. Because of her, I'm convinced I can do anything I put my mind and consistent effort toward. I'm thankful for her prayers, love, and support. To my father, Naurice H. Leigh, Sr., thank you for turning back to "pick up" the 4-year-old little girl who longed for you. In doing so, I was able to understand and get to know the rest of me. To my sisters, Jehreva K. Brown and Jamila A. Brown, thank you for meeting my uncertainty about this book project with encouragement.

I'd like to recognize those who helped me develop something worth sharing with the world. To my editor, who wishes to anonymously add value to the world, one million thanks for your consultation, patience, and encouragement throughout this process. Many thanks to Make Your Mark Publishing Solutions for serving as my independent author consultant. To my friend and business partner, Tiffany R. Nicholson, co-founder of The Muse & The Messenger, LLC, a boutique writing and editing firm, one thousand thanks for your ongoing support. Your candid feedback helped me further develop my thoughts. To my advisor and friend, Dr. Monifa Love, I cherish our relationship. Thank you for your willingness to read and offer feedback. Somehow, you know how to express things verbally that I've thought about but never articulated.

Special thanks is also due to my creative team. To the Be Inspired Global team, many thanks for managing my public relations efforts and for joining my media production team, to include my photographer and videographers.

In addition to the support I received from my family, throughout this process, there were a few people who encouraged me to keep writing. I'd like to acknowledge and thank Dr. Anya Miller Hall, Paulette Samuels Lewis, Laquisha Hall, Lisa Jones Tinch, and Rosalind Haynes, for each of their roles in my life.

Notes

INTRODUCTION

Geiger, A.W., and Gretchen Livingston. "8 Facts about Love and Marriage in America." Pew Research Center. Pew Research Center, February 13, 2019. https://www.pewresearch.org/fact-tank/2019/02/13/8-facts-about-love-and-marriage/.

Stepler, Renee. "Number of Cohabiting Americans Rises, Especially among Those 50+." Pew Research Center. Pew Research Center, April 6, 2017. https://www.pewresearch.org/fact-tank/2017/04/06/number-of-u-s-adults-cohabiting-with-a-partner-continues-to-rise-especially-among-those-50-and-older/.

1: SLEEPING BEAUTY

Jatlaoui, MD, Tara C., Lindsay Eckhaus, MPH, Michele G. Mandel, Antoinette Nguyen, MD, Titilope Oduyebo, MD, Emily Petersen, MD, and Maura K. Whiteman, PhD. "Abortion Surveillance - United States, 2016."

Centers for Disease Control and Prevention. Centers for Disease Control and Prevention, November 27, 2019. https://www.cdc.gov/mmwr/volumes/68/ss/ss6811a1.htm.

2: OH WHERE, OH WHERE IS BOAZ?

Chapman, Gary D. "Things I Wish I'd Known before We Got Married." Introduction. In Things I Wish I'd Known before We Got Married, 10. Chicago, IL: Northfield Pub., 2010.

4: MOONLIGHT PATH

Romero, Angelita D., Oralla P. Biteng, Rene C. Romero, Potenciana D.C. Cruz, and Lydia P. Lalunio. "Phases of the Moon." Essay. In Science and Health, 4th ed., 156. Manila, Philippines: Rex Bookstore, 1993.

5: A SCREAM SAVED MY LIFE

Fogel, Alan. "Emotional and Physical Pain Activate Similar Brain Regions." Psychology Today. Sussex Publishers, April 19, 2012. https://www.psychologytoday.com/us/blog/body-sense/201204/emotional-and-physical-pain-activate-similar-brain-regions.

Weir, Kirsten. "The Pain of Social Rejection." Monitor on Psychology. American Psychological Association, 2012. https://www.apa.org/monitor/2012/04/rejection.